W9-BZL-891

AFTER EASTER

How Christ's Resurrection
Changed Everything

AFTER EASTER

How Christ's Resurrection
Changed Everything

JEREMY ROYAL HOWARD
+ DOUG POWELL

HOLMAN
REFERENCE

NASHVILLE, TENNESSEE

After Easter: How Christ's Resurrection Changed Everything

© Copyright 2015 by Jeremy Royal Howard and Doug Powell

B&H Publishing Group

All rights reserved.

ISBN 978-1-4336-0816-2

Dewey Decimal Classification: 232.97
Subject Heading: JESUS CHRIST—RESURRECTION / JESUS
CHRIST—APPEARANCES / SALVATION

Unless otherwise stated all Scripture quotations are from the *Holman
Christian Standard Bible*® Copyright 1999, 2000, 2002, 2003, 2009 by
Holman Bible Publishers. Used by permission.

Printed in China
1 2 3 4 5 6 7 8 9 10 · 20 19 18 17 16 15
DBS

CONTENTS

CHAPTER 1

THE REIGN OF DEATH

WHEN YOU THINK OF CHRISTMAS, what comes to mind? Family? Snow? Presents? Baby Jesus? Those are some obvious answers, but what about curse? Death? Punishment? Christmas should make you think of these things as well.

Too often we think of Jesus's birth as a quaint nativity scene and nothing more. We envision a beautiful baby, the centerpiece of a hay-strewn floor in a rustic room aglow with lantern light. The animals have gathered to warm themselves and behold the child. We see Jesus's parents also, simple and earnest folk, kneeling at his manger. They're aware that their child is special, but they don't yet grasp the fullness of it. All of this is true enough, but there's something more.

That something more is a human problem so profound that no mere human—no matter how wise or strong or upright—could ever hope to solve it. The solution required nothing less than divine intervention, action on an infinite scale. How would God move? By sending an angel army? By rolling up the sky like a scroll? No, none of that.

He sent a baby.

The feel-good scene of the nativity was Jesus's first step in fixing the human problem, a fix that would involve his eventual humiliation, torture, and public execution on a cross. This violent end wasn't ill fate or a tragic mix-up; neither was it simply miscarried justice. No, God the Father *planned* Jesus's sacrificial mission before the creation of the world, and Jesus began to accomplish that mission from the moment of his birth as the one born both human and divine.

What was required of Jesus was perfection from start to finish. No sin, no moral slackness, no self-centeredness. He was to live a blameless human life, adhering always to God's law. He had to get right what Adam and Eve and every human after them got so tragically wrong. Only by this standard would Jesus be fit for the task given him. And so it is that Christmas began the work that was completed on Easter morning.

☩

The world wasn't tainted when God created it. It was pristine, pure, unmarred by sin. God called all he made "good" (Genesis 1:4,10,12,18,21,25), and when he created Adam and Eve on day six he upped his assessment and said it was all "very good" (Genesis 1:31). Creation at that time was an undimmed reflection of God's nature. This included Adam and Eve, who were created in the likeness of God. They had pure hearts that were able to obey God and love him without deviation. Today we can't even imagine having that kind of purity. What makes their situation even more incredible is that they were told *not* to do only one thing. The focus of God's instructions was on all the good things they were given to do:

> Be fruitful, multiply, fill the earth, and subdue it.
> Rule the fish of the sea, the birds of the sky, and
> every creature that crawls on the earth.
>
> GENESIS 1:28

What privilege! These aren't just things Adam and Eve *could* and *should* do; these are things they would *want* to do. Sure, the assignments entailed hard work and planning, but these can be some of our best sources of joy. Adam and Eve were given the chance to be nothing less than world builders, stewards over a vast domain teeming with possibilities for culture and grandeur and contentment. There was abundance to be had, delights from the hand of the Creator who set Adam and Eve up as the centerpieces of his work.

> Look, I have given you every seed-bearing plant on the surface of the entire earth and every tree whose fruit contains seed. This food will be for you, for all the wildlife of the earth, for every bird of the sky, and for every creature that crawls on the earth—everything having the breath of life in it. I have given every green plant for food.
>
> GENESIS 1:29-30

Besides providing for their every need and giving them a variety of opportunities, God gave himself. Adam and Eve were permitted to be in his immediate presence, innocent souls communing with Holy God. All of this benefit came with only one restriction: Adam and Eve were not to eat the fruit of the tree of the knowledge of good and evil (Genesis 2:17).

The ban on this fruit doesn't mean the tree was bad, and neither does it mean God was keeping them from the best. They were given every other tree and plant to eat from and enjoy. Instead, God banned them from this tree as a kind of test or probationary period. It wasn't an impossible task. Adam and Eve, unfallen and pure of heart, had the power to obey God and keep his *one* restriction.

This command wasn't about the tree, really. It was about placing God at the center of all thinking and the foundation of all knowledge. God is the Maker of all things that can be known and all the ways they can be known. The command aimed to teach them to rely on him and nothing else. Without God as the foundation of life, there can only be death. This is why God tells them, "But you must not eat from the tree of the knowledge of good and evil, for on the day you eat from it, you will certainly die" (Genesis 2:17).

With all of this understood and set before their unclouded minds, Adam and Eve chose to disobey. It goes down as the most shocking choice in history. God had given them millions of joyful "do's" and only one simple "don't," and yet they chose the "don't." By this act they put themselves in the place of God. They made themselves judges over him, deciding that they knew better than he.

Satan was of course the originator of this tactic. Now he coaxed Adam and Eve into adopting it by asking, "Did God really say, 'You can't eat from any tree in the garden?'" (Genesis 3:1). This questions God, but by what standard can God be questioned? God made all things that exist outside of himself; he grounds the standards of truth, right and wrong, and the laws of logic. Try to operate outside of the things made possible by God and you literally cannot think a coherent thought or any thought at all.

After questioning God's authority, Satan continued his temptation by saying there would be no consequences, that disobeying God wouldn't lead to death.

"No! You will not die," the serpent said to the woman. "In fact, God knows that when you eat it

THE REIGN OF DEATH

your eyes will be opened and you will be like God,
knowing good and evil."

GENESIS 3:4-5

With just a bite everything changed. Adam and Eve didn't drop dead immediately, but they did die a more fateful death: death of the spirit to God. Physical life ends in a grave because spiritual life is a graveyard from the start. The most vital part of Adam and Eve, the ability of their souls to fellowship freely with God, was destroyed in the instant of their disobedience. Innocence was replaced by insurmountable guilt, purity exchanged for twisted motives. They had been created with a nature that made them able not to sin, able to remain in communion with God forever. Sadly they chose to throw all of that away in a bid for something falsely billed as better.

Spiritual death tainted their core identities. They went from being able not to sin to being unable not to sin. Perfect obedience to God was now impossible; even acts of obedience became tainted with self-concern and a sense of striving for favor. Adam and Eve could never do what God required of them. And because disobedience tainted their nature, they passed this spiritual death down to all their offspring—you, me, *everyone*.

All of us are born spiritually dead. Infants don't understand right from wrong, but the fallennesss is in them from the start, an automatic inheritance coming down through the generations. Give it a short while and it proves itself, for without exception we make sinful choices as we grow in our moral comprehension. Some hypothesize that we become sinful because we make sinful choices, as if we mark up our pure souls with each wrong act, but the Bible puts it the other way around: we sin because we have a sinful nature. The marring is there from the outset. King David makes this clear:

> "Indeed, I was guilty when I was born; I was sinful when my mother conceived me."
>
> PSALM 51:5

The Apostle Paul agrees and shows just how powerfully our sinful natures grip us:

> There is no one righteous, not even one.
> There is no one who understands;
> there is no one who seeks God.
> All have turned away;
> all alike have become useless.
> There is no one who does what is good,
> not even one.
>
> ROMANS 3:10-12

Sometimes we think we can outweigh our sin if we pile up more good things than bad. We strive to tip the scales and win God's approval. This is what almost all religions inspire people to do. The problem is that sin is so abhorrent to God, so counter to his divine nature, that even one sin deserves eternal punishment. Shall the finite creature strike against the infinite Creator and incur no penalty? The standard required by God is perfection, not a majority of good actions. If you stop at every stop sign except one, you still deserve punishment for running the one. Sin is the same but with infinitely worse consequences. When you sin, you've not offended a finite ruler who set forth a circumstantial law; you've offended an infinite Ruler who set forth laws reflecting his infinite nature.

Even the things we do that are good by worldly standards are corrupted by sinful motives. According to Jesus, we can do nothing without him (John 15:5). There's no true good we can do by our own abilities. And because sin is our nature, it touches every part of us. We aren't as evil as we could possibly be, but there's nothing about us that sin hasn't tainted.

Sin in any degree keeps us from deserving God's affection. As Paul says, "For the wages of sin is death" (Romans 6:23). He doesn't say how much sin; *any* sin is enough. Period. The result of Adam's sin is that death reigns. It grips us all.

Death also grips creation. The "very good" world that God created is under the curse of sin, just as we are. We see the effects of sin all around us. Natural disasters, disease, famine, illnesses, birth defects—these and other natural tragedies are the effects of sin. The reign of death encompasses our world, our nature, our abilities, and our thoughts.

That storied manger in Bethlehem cradled a child not just virgin born but *perfect* born. Jesus lived the life of obedience required of us, and rather than clear his path of all troubles, his righteousness earned him the cross, an assignment from the Father to suffer the death penalty against a stray human race. Hanging there—pierced, bleeding, *innocent*—Jesus received the full measure of God's wrath for our sins. As he did that for us, his righteousness and perfect obedience were credited to us as if they were our own. Through faith in him we are judged to be perfect. Apart from faith in him, we're left owing an everlasting penalty.

AFTER EASTER

But what good can a Savior do if he's dead and buried? Has death not defeated him also, the same as it has every last one of Adam's race? As we'll see in the next chapter, death's death certificate was signed the moment a tomb cracked open outside Jerusalem and set free one whom death couldn't hold.

REFLECT AND DISCUSS

1. The Bible teaches that humans are made in God's image and that the earth is ours to steward and govern as his representatives. How does this exalted view of humanity compare to the view you have held? Explain how the views you hear expressed in culture, media, and education are different from the Bible's. How do the differing views impact our choices and sense of purpose?

2. Satan's tactic with Adam and Eve was to make them question God's truthfulness. In what ways has Satan tried this in your life? What lessons have you learned, both from falling for his tactic and from resisting it?

3. Do you think of your sins as being infinitely bad, or do you feel that they are understandable and God will overlook them? How does your view compare to the Bible's view?

4. The Bible teaches that we are born dead in our sins and can't please God with any of our good behavior. Are you trusting in your works or in the work of Christ to save you?

5. Since death is a result of sin, it is important that we discuss the issue with family and friends. Do you talk to others about their need for a Savior? What are some approaches you can use to start these conversations?

CHAPTER 2

THE SON RISES

JESUS'S RESURRECTION FROM THE DEAD is not the cause of a believer's forgiveness; our forgiveness was secured when Jesus accepted on the cross the wrath that was owed to us. His perfect obedience was credited to us at Calvary on Friday, not Sunday morning in a vacant tomb. In this light, have people exaggerated the importance of the resurrection?

The claims made about Jesus's achievement on the cross are extraordinary, and that's why the resurrection is so important. All the things Jesus taught about his identity and purpose, as well as his predictions that he would rise from the dead on the third day, were validated when he rose up from the tomb. Alive again and forever, he's a sure guide in all he ever said or did.

Jesus taught many things that couldn't be fact-checked, but he also performed many miracles and signs to show that he was telling the truth. Take the following episode for example:

Seeing their faith He said, "Friend, your sins are forgiven you."
Then the scribes and the Pharisees began to think: "Who is this man who
speaks blasphemies? Who can forgive sins but God alone? "
But perceiving their thoughts, Jesus replied to them, "Why are you thinking

this in your hearts? Which is easier: to say, 'Your
sins are forgiven you,'
or to say, 'Get up and walk'? But so you may
know that the Son of Man has
authority on earth to forgive sins"—He told the
paralyzed man, "I tell you:
Get up, pick up your mat, and go home."

LUKE 5:20-24

By miraculously healing the man's visible physical state, Jesus gave
compelling evidence for his power to heal the man's invisible spiritual state. Similarly, the resurrection is evidence that Jesus can be
trusted about his teachings and claims. A man claiming to be God
should be dismissed outright, unless he's raising people from the
dead (Lazarus in John 11, Jarius's daughter in Mark 5, a widow's son
in Luke 7), walking on water and calming storms (Matthew 14),
healing lepers and the blind (Luke 17–18; John 9), and coming to
life again after execution (Matthew 28; Luke 24; John 20). If there
had been no resurrection, there would be no Christianity today or
any reason for it to have started in the first place. The Apostle Paul
makes this point:

Now if Christ is proclaimed as raised from the
dead, how can some of you say, "There is no
resurrection of the dead"? But if there is no
resurrection of the dead, then Christ has not been
raised; and if Christ has not been raised, then
our proclamation is without foundation, and so
is your faith. In addition, we are found to be false

THE SON RISES

> witnesses about God, because we have testified
> about God that He raised up Christ—whom He
> did not raise up if in fact the dead are not raised.
> For if the dead are not raised, Christ has not
> been raised. And if Christ has not been raised,
> your faith is worthless; you are still in your sins.
> Therefore, those who have fallen asleep in Christ
> have also perished. If we have put our hope in
> Christ for this life only, we should be pitied more
> than anyone.
>
> 1 CORINTHIANS 15:12-17

This passage is unique in the scripture of world religions because it points out what you have to disprove if you want to debunk the religion. If Jesus did not rise from the dead, Christianity is false. Simple as that. But Paul is so certain of the evidence for Jesus's resurrection that he has no problem admitting that everything hinges on it. He *wants* people to examine the resurrection evidence, not just take it on blind faith or believe against reason. Why would he take this stance? Because the evidence is powerful and persuasive.

There are many New Testament scholars in the world, and not all of them approach their studies with openness to faith. Some even choose to specialize in New Testament studies for the purpose of undermining the Bible's claims. Despite all the diversity of scholarly motivations and viewpoints, around a dozen Christian claims pertaining to Jesus's crucifixion and aftermath are accepted by virtually all New Testament scholars regardless of their religious beliefs. These facts are supported in multiple sources, including non-Christian sources dating from the first and second centuries.

AFTER EASTER

Scholars who reject the resurrection have to explain what happened to Jesus in a way that takes stock of the widely accepted facts; otherwise they're just ducking out of sight instead of facing evidence that runs counter to their antiresurrection views. Of the many skeptical theories, none make sense of the dozen widely accepted facts. Even if we reduce the dozen facts by half, the alternate theories still can't make sense of them all.

This "minimal facts argument" is a powerful tool for defending Jesus's resurrection because the defender of the resurrection isn't even using all of the powerful evidences and arguments available to him. Instead, he agrees to use only a handful of the facts that non-Christian scholars and even Bible critics and atheists accept. Essentially tying one hand behind his back, the defender of Jesus's resurrection is still able to show that Jesus's literal resurrection is the best explanation for the factuality of the "minimal facts."

So what are the minimal facts? They can be stated, in an unbiased way that doesn't tilt the argument in favor of resurrection, as follows:

Jesus was crucified. This isn't disputed. Jesus's crucifixion was sometimes described as being hung on a tree, but that's a reference to the wood of the cross, not an alternate account of his execution. Without question Jesus suffered torture and execution on a cross, a common fate for those convicted of crimes in the Roman era.

Jesus died. Sharpshooters may miss, and the hangman may foul up the noose, but crucifixion was a sure death conducted by professional executioners. There's only one account of someone surviving crucifixion, and that person was taken down almost immediately after being placed on the cross. It was a quick reversal that saved a life, not a botched crucifixion. The one major historical attempt to deny that Jesus died is known as the swoon theory, and it has never garnered serious support because it hypothesizes that Jesus suffered the lashings, crucifixion, and spear through the side (without flinching), and yet survived and was able without assistance to unwrap his burial cloths, roll away the two-ton tomb stone from inside the tomb, and convincingly present himself as able-bodied, whole, and divine!

Jesus was buried in a tomb. A few scholars try to deny Jesus's tomb burial because crucifixion victims were rarely given back to their families for proper burial. Instead, victims were left on the cross to rot and serve as a warning to others, or else the executioners threw them into common graves. The goal of crucifixion was not just to kill but to degrade and teach a lesson. However, the fact that proper burial of crucifixion victims was rare doesn't mean there weren't exceptions, and the evidence for an exception in Jesus's case is, well, *exceptional.* No alternative theory existed in the ancient literature, and the pervasiveness of the empty-tomb theme among believers and unbelievers alike relies on there having been a tomb burial.

Jesus's tomb was found empty three days after his burial. Some skeptics suggest Jesus's followers went to the wrong tomb and thus mistakenly sparked off resurrection belief, but Jewish sources such as the *Toledoth Jesu* (written around AD 500, containing early tradition regarding how non-Christian Jews viewed Jesus) record that the disciples stole Jesus's body from his tomb. Clearly that means non-Christian Jews acknowledged that Jesus's followers went to the correct tomb. Justin Martyr, a Christian theologian who wrote around AD 150, also says non-Christian Jews alleged that Jesus's followers had stolen his body. Further, the New Testament itself says this is what non-Christian Jews taught (Matthew 28:11-15). This means early believers and nonbelievers alike agreed that Jesus was buried and that the tomb—*the correct tomb*—was found empty. Naturally both groups knew the exact tomb Jesus was buried in or else they wouldn't have agreed on the fact that Jesus's tomb was found empty. Nonbelievers thus invented the theft claim in order to deny that the empty tomb indicated a resurrection. The theft claim makes no sense, however, for if nonbelievers *did* steal the body in an attempt to dishearten Jesus's followers or else further degrade his corpse, they would've produced the body right away once they realized their ploy had backfired and created a resurrection rumor. Any idea that *believers* stole Jesus's body in order to create a resurrection hoax fails on several accounts, including the problem of their having to get past the guards at the tomb, and the problem of their paying such a high cost for perpetuating a claim they knew to be false. For decades Christians were ostracized and persecuted. Why stick to your resurrection claims when (1) you know the claims are false, and (2) the claims only cause you suffering?

Followers of Jesus believed they encountered him after his death. Even scholars who disbelieve Jesus's resurrection acknowledge that his earliest followers were convinced they had seen him alive again after his death. People who thought they saw and spoke to the risen Jesus include his disciples, followers such as the women at the tomb, the men on the road to Emmaus, at least one skeptic, and a gathering of 500 people. Attempts to argue that these people were mistaken to think they saw the risen Jesus have included allegations of group hallucination (based on religious hype or drug use!) and wishful thinking. It's far-fetched to think a group hallucination could happen even once and lead people to believe in a resurrection, but multiple times, and with hallucinations convincing even committed nonbelievers of Jesus's resurrection (see below)? One has to ask who is doing the wishful thinking here.

Enemies of Jesus believed they encountered him after his death. This is a hard fact to explain for those who deny Jesus's resurrection because an enemy of Jesus or someone who steadfastly disbelieved him would obviously require convincing proof before switching sides. One such enemy was Saul of Tarsus, who became the Apostle Paul. Saul was an educated and committed Pharisee who saw Jesus as a heretic who deserved death. That's why he persecuted Jesus's followers (Acts 8–9). He was on his way to Tarsus when something happened that changed him forever. As a result of an encounter with the risen Jesus, Paul gave up all comfort and privilege and spent the rest of his life spreading resurrection belief all over the Mediterranean world. During that time he was beaten, imprisoned, hungry, shipwrecked, homeless, and according to tradition, beheaded. Did Paul make such a costly life change on the basis of flimsy evidence? If so, wouldn't he have backed out upon further reflection, especially as his new beliefs began to cost him all comfort? The only sensible conclusion is that Paul became a Christian based on what he felt was indisputable evidence.

An even tougher enemy to explain is Jesus's brother James. During Jesus's ministry James didn't believe Jesus (John 7) and thought he was insane (Mark 3). But shortly after Jesus's death, James became a believer. Think about what it would take for you to believe that your own *brother* is God. Talk about a high standard of proof! Against his every expectation, James did come to believe in Jesus and believe so strongly that he became leader of the Jerusalem church. Not only that, he wouldn't budge from his belief even when his life was threatened. Eventually he was killed for his faith, something he wouldn't have allowed had he harbored any doubt that Jesus had risen from the dead.

---------------------- ✝ ----------------------

The resurrection is the only explanation that makes sense of the accepted facts. Paul was willing to rest everything on the resurrection claim because it is an assured fact of history. Are you willing to rest everything on it as well? Will you devote your life to the one who vouched for his claims by coming back from the dead?

AFTER EASTER

REFLECT AND DISCUSS

1. Does the fact that Jesus rose from the dead convince you to accept as true all his teachings and claims? Why or why not?

2. Prior to reading this chapter, how familiar were you with evidence for Jesus's resurrection? Do you feel the evidence shared above will help you engage nonbelievers? How?

3. Many Christians say they accept the resurrection on faith alone. This may sound commendable, but it's a position the Bible itself doesn't take. The Bible emphasizes the factuality of the resurrection of Jesus. How do the facts presented in this chapter change your thinking or your confidence in the resurrection of Jesus? What are some things you might do to become more familiar with the factual grounding of Christian faith?

4. Early Christian confidence in the resurrection was so strong that the church admitted if the resurrection were untrue, then Christianity is untrue. What is the modern church tempted to focus on rather than a confidence in the resurrection? Possible answers might include good things such as teaching moral behavior or social activism.

5. How can you best answer a friend who has doubts about the resurrection of Jesus?

CHAPTER 3

DEATH IS DEFEATED

DEATH IS SO MUCH A PART of daily life that we may fail to realize what an absurd imposition it is. We drive past hospitals and graveyards so often that they become nothing more than background scenes. You pull your clothes out of an antique wardrobe every morning, never once feeling shocked that its builder builds no more. We buy health and life insurance policies and put away money for retirement without realizing how bizarre it is that we spend all this money against unavoidable decline and death.

The doom of death hangs over us all, and yet not one of us can imagine what it means to be dead. Try thinking of it. Draw the curtains on your mind and think no thoughts, feel no emotions, hear no sounds. It's impossible. We are alive, and alive is all we understand. Sleep is no analogy, for imaginations and emotion come to us in our sleep, plus we lie down with every expectation of getting back up. Death is the unthinkable but unshakable fate of us all.

Earlier we saw that God the Father sent God the Son to mend the problem of sin and death. The problem got solved on the cross (where the penalty for sin was meted out), and this solution was proven true in the resurrection (where death was shown to be defeated). Some have thought you can divide the solution from the proof and still have an intact gospel. They say Jesus never rose bodily from the grave, but his spirit came alive again and sparked off resurrection hope. This suggestion has many problems. For example, a merely spiritual resurrection doesn't explain the empty tomb or the report by numerous disciples that they interacted with the risen Jesus. If only Jesus's spirit arose, why was the tomb empty? And how can Jesus's disciples, for a period of forty days and in settings as diverse as large gatherings and private conversations, have mistaken an insubstantial spirit for a substantial body that could walk, talk, eat, and be touched?

A further problem with denying Jesus's bodily resurrection is that a merely spiritual resurrection wouldn't take away our sins, for the wages of sin is not just spiritual death but physical death as well. If payment for sin was made on the cross, then sin's curse (death) is canceled. The bodily resurrection of Jesus is the evidence that he did in fact pay the penalty for our sins. The effect of sin could have no hold on him, and therefore his body could not remain dead. According to Peter, "God raised Him up, ending the pains of death, because it was not possible for Him to be held by it" (Acts 2:24).

It wasn't possible for Jesus to be held by death. He had done on the cross the work required to overturn death, and his resurrection proved it. Death entered the world through sin, and so solving the sin problem solves the death problem.

———————————— ✠ ————————————

Without the bodily resurrection of Jesus, Christianity can't exist (1 Corinthians 15:12-19). So much for spiritual resurrections or any idea that Jesus's resurrection was a fiction that proved useful in spreading hope. If Jesus's remains are anywhere on this earth, we are without hope, dead in our sins, saddled still with a curse we cannot break. But we've seen that the literal, bodily resurrection of Jesus is the one conclusion that's able to account for all of the agreed-upon facts. Thus we have no doubt that our sins are forgiven through the work of God the Son who died and rose again. Death cannot hold us down any more than it held Jesus down.

DEATH IS DEFEATED

God raised up the Lord and will also raise us up
by His power.

1 CORINTHIANS 6:14

We know that the One who raised the Lord Jesus will
raise us also with Jesus and present us with you.

2 CORINTHIANS 4:14

These assurances, written by the Apostle Paul, are nothing innovative. Paul took his cues from Jesus himself, who promised that this would be the impact of his ministry.

"For this is the will of My Father: that everyone
who sees the Son and believes in Him may have
eternal life, and I will raise him up on the last day."

JOHN 6:40

"Anyone who eats My flesh and drinks My blood has
eternal life, and I will raise him up on the last day."

JOHN 6:54

Jesus said to her, "I am the resurrection and the
life. The one who believes in Me, even if he dies,
will live."

JOHN 11:25

AFTER EASTER

Even Jesus wasn't being innovative. The resurrection promise was also woven into the Old Testament witness.

I will ransom them from the power of Sheol.
I will redeem them from death.
Death, where are your barbs?
Sheol, where is your sting?

HOSEA 13:14

Many of those who sleep in the dust
of the earth will awake,
some to eternal life,
and some to shame and eternal contempt.

DANIEL 12:2

But I know my living Redeemer,
and He will stand on the dust at last.
Even after my skin has been destroyed,
yet I will see God in my flesh.
I will see Him myself;
my eyes will look at Him, and not as a stranger.
My heart longs within me.

JOB 19:25-27

How can bodily resurrection of the dead be beyond the power of God when it so closely resembles his initial work of creating humans? Genesis 2:7 says God took dust from the ground and fashioned the first man, Adam. Our future resurrection is a work of God as Creator and Restorer, giving the gift of life so that God may be glorified. The resurrection confirms that God will glorify himself through his creation and especially through the aspect of creation that he created in his image—humanity.

✟

We go on living in a fallen world, and we ourselves contribute to the fallenness after we come to faith. But we mature spiritually and are increasingly being conformed to the image of Christ throughout our lives. Ultimately we are made complete, unable to sin, when we receive our heavenly reward.

> For the trumpet will sound,
> and the dead will be raised incorruptible,
> and we will be changed.
> For this corruptible must be clothed
> with incorruptibility,
> and this mortal must be clothed
> with immortality.
> When this corruptible is clothed
> with incorruptibility,
> and this mortal is clothed
> with immortality . . .
>
> 1 CORINTHIANS 15:52-54

It's not just us who will be made perfect at the end times. Creation itself will be perfected. When death entered the world, it did more than change the nature of human beings; it changed the nature of the world itself.

AFTER EASTER

And He said to Adam, "Because you listened to
your wife's voice and ate from the tree about
which I commanded you, 'Do not eat from it':
The ground is cursed because of you.
You will eat from it by means of painful labor
all the days of your life.
It will produce thorns and thistles for you,
and you will eat the plants of the field.
You will eat bread by the sweat of your brow
until you return to the ground,
since you were taken from it.
For you are dust,
and you will return to dust."

GENESIS 3:17-19

Sin and death put the world under a curse, impacting everything. The provision of the earth is abundant, and there's a vast variety of ways it gives us all we need. Still, creation is muted and limping under the weight of sin, yearning for restoration. As Jeremiah said, "How long will the land mourn and the grass of every field wither?" (Jeremiah 12:4). Paul takes Jeremiah's question even further:

For the creation eagerly waits with anticipation
for God's sons to be revealed. For the creation
was subjected to futility—not willingly, but
because of Him who subjected it—in the hope

DEATH IS DEFEATED

that the creation itself will also be set free from
the bondage of corruption into the glorious
freedom of God's children. For we know that the
whole creation has been groaning together with
labor pains until now. And not only that, but we
ourselves who have the Spirit as the firstfruits—
we also groan within ourselves, eagerly waiting
for adoption, the redemption of our bodies.

ROMANS 8:19-23

Just as we groan to be free of death and the effects of sin, creation longs to be remade and set free. The only way to repeal the effects of sin and death is for sin to be paid for and death to be conquered. That's what Jesus came to do, and as a result creation itself will be set free.

"For I will create a new heaven and a new earth;
the past events will not be remembered
or come to mind."

ISAIAH 65:17

Heaven must welcome Him until the times of the
restoration of all things, which God spoke about
by the mouth of His holy prophets from the
beginning.

ACTS 3:21

AFTER EASTER

> But based on His promise, we wait for the new
> heavens and a new earth, where righteousness
> will dwell.
>
> 2 PETER 3:13

Jesus took his lifetime record of perfect obedience and the merit it earned and credited it to us so that we can be judged by his righteous works rather than by our sins. By his resurrection he proved that he accomplished these things. His work is finished. Death is defeated.

> Death has been swallowed up in victory.
> Death, where is your victory?
> Death, where is your sting?
> Now the sting of death is sin,
> and the power of sin is the law.
> But thanks be to God, who gives us the victory
> through our Lord Jesus Christ!
>
> 1 CORINTHIANS 15:54-57

Reflect and Discuss

1. How do we answer the argument that Jesus's resurrection was only spiritual and not bodily? Why does it make such a difference to focus on the physical resurrection of Jesus?

2. How does God's emphasis on his own glory serve to give you confidence in your salvation and God's promises?

DEATH IS DEFEATED

3. The Bible teaches that at our resurrection we will be made complete, unable to sin. One mark of a spiritually maturing believer is that this aspect of resurrection life is one of your greatest anticipations. What actions can you take to increase your anticipation for the future resurrection? How can increasing your anticipation affect your current relationship with God?

4. What are some evidences you see that creation itself needs restoration?

5. Everyday life demands our attention, and focusing on eternity can be difficult. What are some ways you foster an eternal focus in your daily life?

CHAPTER 4

SALVATION THROUGH FAITH

FAITH IS A SLIPPERY WORD TODAY. Often it's used to mean nothing more than wishing. We have this "faith" in our favorite teams, the weather for Saturday, or the outcome of an exam we didn't prepare for. Sometimes we muster up faith as a last resort when life's a tough climb, but this faith disappears just as soon as our road smooths out. Faith is also used as shorthand for the power of positive thinking. Think of how many times you've heard people say, "You just have to have faith in yourself!" When used of religion, faith is often equated with *blind* faith, where you check your mind at the door and accept something you know makes no sense.

One of the challenges when translating the Bible is that there isn't always a word in your language that has exactly the same meaning as the word in the biblical language. That can make it hard for the author's meaning to come through in just the way he intended. Further complicating the translation task is the fact that every language changes over time. For example, think of the ways *cool* and *hot* now have a broader range of meaning than was the case in earlier English. A sun-baked sports car is cool. What?

In the case of the word *faith*, both of these translation challenges come into play. The biblical word translated as "faith" doesn't easily translate into English, plus the meaning of the English word has shifted over time. As a result, *faith*, as many of us understand it, doesn't convey the same meaning as the biblical word for *faith*.

The Greek word in the New Testament that is translated as faith is *pistis*. It means "trust, firm persuasion, or conviction." What do you need in order to be persuaded? Reasons. And what do you need to become convicted of something? You need evidence. Our culture's idea of faith doesn't include reason or evidence. Those things aren't needed to make a wish, but they are needed for trust. Unfortunately, sometimes even Christians think of reason and evidence as actually being contrary to faith, as if having faith without reasons or evidence makes it more pure in some way, more pleasing to God. But the truth is that without reasons and evidence you can't have biblical faith; you just have wishful thinking.

Wishes and faith are essentially polar opposites. Wishes are about the person doing the believing. When you tell me what you wish for, I don't learn about the true value of the money you wish you had, the beauty or fame you long for, or the friends you hope to gain. Instead, I learn about your heart. You describe for me the things you feel will make you complete, and so I form an understanding of your insecurities and the things upon which you build your identity.

Faith—defined biblically—points in the opposite direction of a wish. Faith points at the value of its object. If you tell me you have faith that the bridge will hold the weight of your car, the focus isn't on you but on the merits of the bridge. Is it worthy of your faith? Is it built and maintained well? If you put your faith in something that isn't true, then your faith is worthless no matter how sincerely you believe it. Believing a lie doesn't make it true, and truth is true even if no one believes it.

In light of how the Bible defines *faith*, you can see why no one is saved just because their faith is sincere. You can sincerely place your faith in a sham or a hoax or a misinterpreted claim. In biblical teaching, sincerity of faith is of course necessary for salvation, but faith's sincerity isn't the reason we're saved. We're saved because of the truthfulness of what we rest our faith in, claims including:

- We are hopeless sinners guilty before God.
- Jesus, God's Son, died to pay for our sins.
- Jesus lived a life of perfect obedience that is credited to us through faith.
- Jesus rose from the dead, proving true his work on the cross.

What does Christianity have that other religions don't? Interestingly, the answer isn't Jesus. Major religions and worldviews often have a place for Jesus, sometimes even a certain "faith" in Jesus. Well, faith in a *variety* of Jesus, anyway. Atheists typically admire Jesus as long as he's presented merely as a good human teacher and an example of how to live against the dominant religious grain. Muslims regard Jesus as a prophet and have respect for him. Mormons have even more respect for Jesus, but they also believe we can become divine, truly equal to Jesus. Atheism, Islam, and Mormonism have different ideas about the human problem and how to fix it and certainly different views about God and the world, but their common tactic is to use human works to fix the human problem. Whether by the efforts of science and education or by the efforts of adhering to religious rules and claims of revelation, these worldviews teach that salvation comes through our own efforts. Follow the rules, obey the steps, hear the prophet, and it'll turn out OK.

Christianity is the only religion that teaches that salvation is by grace, a gift freely given by the very God whom we've offended. Because the moral standard required by God is perfection, there's no way we can pay for our sins. We can't take our fragmented, broken souls—*dead* souls—and make them alive or whole again. There are no works we can do to earn salvation, and even our best acts fall short.

SALVATION THROUGH FAITH

All of us have become like something unclean,
and all our righteous acts are like
a polluted garment;
all of us wither like a leaf,
and our iniquities carry us away like the wind.

ISAIAH 64:6

There is no one righteous, not even one.
There is no one who understands;
there is no one who seeks God.
All have turned away;
all alike have become useless.
There is no one who does what is good,
not even one.

ROMANS 3:10-12, QUOTING PSALM 53:3

For all have sinned and fall short
of the glory of God.

ROMANS 3:23

And you were dead in your trespasses and sins.

EPHESIANS 2:1

God didn't have to save anyone. He would be justified in con-
signing everyone to eternal punishment. But instead he gave us
something we don't deserve: himself.

AFTER EASTER

The work of Christ isn't just automatically applied without any responsibility or action on our part. If it were, all people—Christ followers, Christ deniers, those indifferent to Christ, those ignorant of Christ—would be saved. That isn't the Bible's message. There's urgency to spreading the gospel, and each person must choose between life and death, belief and unbelief. Christ's saving work is applied only to those who hear the gospel and respond in faith, accepting that Christ is the Son of God who won their salvation on the cross.

But God, who is rich in mercy, because of His great love that He had for us, made us alive with the Messiah even though we were dead in trespasses. You are saved by grace! . . . For you are saved by grace through faith, and this is not from yourselves; it is God's gift.

EPHESIANS 2:4-5,8

For while we were still helpless, at the appointed moment, Christ died for the ungodly. . . . But God proves His own love for us in that while we were still sinners, Christ died for us! Much more then, since we have now been declared righteous by His blood, we will be saved through Him from wrath. For if, while we were enemies, we were reconciled to God through the death of His Son, then how much more, having been reconciled, will we be saved by His life! And not only that, but we also rejoice in God through our Lord Jesus

SALVATION THROUGH FAITH

Christ. We have now received this reconciliation
through Him.

ROMANS 5:6,8-10

By His own choice, He gave us a new birth by
the message of truth so that we would be the
firstfruits of His creatures.

JAMES 1:18

As the writer of Hebrews says, Jesus is "the source and perfecter of our faith" (Hebrews 12:2). Some translations say he's the "author" of our faith. How amazing is that? That God would give people who have rebelled against him a way to be forgiven and also the faith to believe it is a goodness we'll never fully comprehend. In fact, we sometimes find it too good to be true, and we fall into trying to earn God's favor or contribute to our salvation in some way. Down this path lies only trouble. Working to contribute to our salvation is working against the finished, sufficient work of Christ. It constitutes a denial of the gospel message: Jesus came to do for us what we're unable to do. It also resembles original sin, for by importing our good acts into the equation, we're trying to make ourselves equal to (as good as) God. Nothing could be more futile.

The opposite error is also a danger: thinking that it doesn't matter how we live because as sinners saved by grace our salvation is secure and our works contribute nothing to it. This attitude is a terrible insult (at the very least) to the profound sacrifice of Christ. It treats grace cheaply and in some cases is used as a license to sin freely without fear of consequence.

AFTER EASTER

We're saved by grace through faith, but that doesn't set aside the need to do good works. Rather than conform to the world, we're called to be conformed to the image of Jesus (see Romans 8:29). Our good works don't serve to complete our salvation or make it stick. Rather, they're the *response* to our complete and sure salvation, evidence of a changed nature, a heart given to God. So essential is this changed nature and the good works that flow from it that the absence of good works indicates absence of true salvation. Jesus's brother says it this way:

> In the same way faith, if it doesn't have works, is dead by itself. . . . You see that a man is justified by works and not by faith alone. . . . For just as the body without the spirit is dead, so also faith without works is dead.
>
> JAMES 2:17,24,26

In the end we actually *are* saved by works—not ours but those of Christ. And one of the works of Christ is the gift of faith itself. As a result of that faith, Paul can declare of believers:

> They are justified freely by His grace through the redemption that is in Christ Jesus. God presented Him as a propitiation through faith in His blood, to demonstrate His righteousness, because in His restraint God passed over the sins previously committed. God presented Him to demonstrate His righteousness at the present time, so that He

would be righteous and declare righteous the one
who has faith in Jesus.

ROMANS 3:24-26

Therefore, since we have been declared righteous
by faith, we have peace with God through our
Lord Jesus Christ. We have also obtained access
through Him by faith into this grace in which we
stand, and we rejoice in the hope of the glory
of God.

ROMANS 5:1-2

Salvation through faith rather than through our good works is an important part of what makes the good news so good. The impossibility of earning salvation through our works condemns us, but it also puts us in a position to admit our hopelessness and accept the Savior who came for us. That is news we should want to share with everyone we meet.

REFLECT AND DISCUSS

1. What is the difference between wishing for something good to happen and having faith as the Bible describes it? How has this chapter enhanced your view of faith?

2. What is the relationship between these words: *wishing, faith, opinion*, and *truth*?

3. What are some evidences that come to mind when you think of the factual grounding for your faith? Why are these particular evidences compelling to you?

4. The key to Jesus's fitness for being our substitute on the cross is the fact that he lived a sinless life, pleasing the Father in all he did. Jesus's works are accounted as our own works through our faith in him. What is your heartfelt reaction to knowing that God the Father desired to save you through the work of Jesus? How does it change your outlook and inform your daily choices?

5. How do we stumble into thinking that good deeds play a role in saving us? What is the implication for non-Christians who trust in good works to save them from God's judgment?

6. What is the relationship between faith in Jesus and doing good works?

CHAPTER 5

THE CHURCH IS BORN

JESUS'S DEATH AND RESURRECTION marked the death of death as well as the rebirth of life. His work on our behalf makes spiritual rebirth possible, and many Christians mark the day they came to faith as their most significant birthday, their *spiritual* birthday. It's a new beginning that never ends.

Unfortunately, some Christians fail to make the best of the gift they've been given. Mimicking our culture's individualism, they strike out on their own and practice Lone Ranger Christianity. They don't connect with other believers or get involved in the work of God in a local church. They act as though their faith is a private project—a self-improvement program—rather than part of a far bigger movement that spans not just human history but the horizons of time and eternity.

When you became a believer, you weren't abandoned at (re)birth and left to make it on your own. God went to extraordinary lengths to save you when you were his outright enemy; shall he set you aside and watch you struggle now that you're called by his name? Of course not, and yet many Christians exile themselves from God's care and try to make it on their own in a world hostile to God.

When we come to faith, we're joined to a community built by God, the church. Fellow believers of every variety become your family, your brothers and sisters in Christ. The church isn't a building; Jesus didn't come to establish a franchise chain or erect ornate structures. When Paul writes, "Christ loved the church and gave Himself for her" (Ephesians 5:25), he's talking about *people*. The church is made of all those who believe in the work of

AFTER EASTER

Christ—not just believers alive now but those in the past as well. We have a huge family, a rich community gathered by God himself across time and culture. Our beliefs are personal insomuch as we ourselves are responsible for them, but those same core beliefs are shared all over the world and back through time to the founding of the church in the wake of Jesus's resurrection. In this light you are not your own; you belong to Christ and his Church.

What did the church look like in the beginning? Just a few weeks after Jesus's resurrection, about 120 believers regularly met and prayed (Acts 1:14-15), bound together by a common faith and a radical new identity. They had encountered the risen Christ and could never go back to thinking or living the same as before. Do you suppose any of them attempted to go it alone after witnessing the miracle of resurrection? No, they banded together, inseparably united around an amazing truth. The New Testament word translated as "church" is *ekklesia*. It means "assembly" or "gathering." Early Christians did life together, cared for one another, prayed together, and grew together in holiness and the knowledge of God. God used that community to catch the attention of the world and grow the body of believers.

Fifty days after the crucifixion, the Father sent the Holy Spirit to the church. Immediately the number of believers exploded. Jews from all over the world were living in Jerusalem, and many others were visiting for Pentecost. When the Spirit descended on the believers, they were miraculously granted the ability to speak all sorts of foreign languages. A crowd gathered to see the spectacle. People from Rome, Crete, Egypt, Persia, and elsewhere heard their own languages being spoken by uneducated Galilean Jews. Recognizing the power of the sign God had given, Peter stood and delivered a sermon that led 3,000 people to faith (Acts 2:41). Word spread quickly then. God was doing something special through the followers of Jesus, and their message was a message of hope offered to all people regardless of their social status, gender, nationality, or any other measurement. Eternal life was offered to all, and daily more and more embraced it (v. 42).

Because these new Christians were from all over the known world, they spread Christian faith into new territories when they went home from Jerusalem. Empowered by a hopeful message and signs from God, they sought to rescue the world from judgment.

<hr>

The first book in the New Testament wasn't written until 15 to 20 years after Jesus rose from the dead, and it was another few decades before all of the books were complete. In the absence of God-given writings, how did early Christians know what to believe? Did they all believe the same thing? When differences of opinion arose, how did believers choose which path to follow? The answer is that they had creeds to guide them.

Creeds are short statements of faith that can easily be memorized. They're summaries of Christian theology that contain the core teachings. Before the New Testament was written, as many as three dozen creeds were in use that expressed the same basic beliefs. We know this because the creeds are quoted in the New Testament. We can know what the early church believed by looking at the creeds. Take for example 1 Corinthians 15:3-7, which quotes a creed so old it probably dates from within one or two years of the resurrection. This passage affirms:

> . . . that Christ died for our sins
> according to the Scriptures,
> that He was buried,
> that He was raised on the third day

according to the Scriptures,
and that He appeared to Cephas,
then to the Twelve.
Then He appeared to over 500 brothers at one time;
most of them are still alive,
but some have fallen asleep.
Then He appeared to James,
then to all the apostles.

This statement is powerful, compact, and packed with theology. Creeds were adaptable in the sense that new information could be added as the church faced new questions and challenges. Looking at several of the early creeds in the New Testament, we can bring their elements together and outline the following early beliefs:

- There is only one God, immortal, eternal, Creator of all things.
- God is three persons (Father, Son, and Holy Spirit) in one Godhead.
- Jesus is God manifest in the flesh.
- Jesus is Lord, Messiah, the Holy One of God, the Son of Man, and the Son of God through whom we exist.
- Jesus was from Nazareth and a descendant of David.
- Jesus was betrayed.
- Jesus appeared before Pontus Pilate.
- Jesus was buried and crucified.
- Jesus was resurrected from the dead on the third day after his burial.
- Jesus appeared to his disciples and many followers after his death.
- Jesus ascended into heaven.

THE CHURCH IS BORN

- Jesus died for our sins and was raised for our justification.
- Salvation is through belief in Jesus alone.
- Jesus was the fulfillment of Old Testament prophecy.

✛

The church isn't just a community that cares for one another and accepts a core set of beliefs. It also exists for the worship of God and the exercise of spiritual gifts for the betterment of others. Here are some of the verses touching on these purposes:

Every day they devoted themselves to meeting together in the temple complex, and broke bread from house to house. They ate their food with a joyful and humble attitude, praising God and having favor with all the people.

ACTS 2:46-47

Let the message about the Messiah dwell richly among you, teaching and admonishing one another in all wisdom, and singing psalms, hymns, and spiritual songs, with gratitude in your hearts to God.

COLOSSIANS 3:16

And let us be concerned about one another in order to promote love and good works, not staying away from our worship meetings, as some habitually do, but encouraging each other, and all the more as you see the day drawing near.

HEBREWS 10:24-25

AFTER EASTER

Now all the believers were together and held all
things in common. They sold their possessions
and property and distributed the proceeds to all,
as anyone had a need.

ACTS 2:44-45

What about people who attend church but aren't believers? Sailing under a false flag goes all the way back to Christian beginnings, when Judas posed as a disciple of Jesus. To address the issue of non-Christians in the church, theologians distinguish between the visible church and the invisible church. The visible church is everyone who identifies as Christian. Everyone in this group is "visible" because this group is defined as those who regularly attend. Among this group, sadly, are those who are imposters or self-deceived. The invisible church (the true church) is "invisible" because they are a subset of the visible church, and the fact they are truly saved is known by God, who is never fooled by religious posturing that may mislead others about the true spiritual state of a person. The fact that some church attendees aren't genuine Christians doesn't mean we should look at everyone with suspicion. We should consider each profession of faith charitably and recognize that there's no better place for unbelievers to be than in the midst of those who truly believe.

✝

Sometimes we think of the church as something that began to exist only after Christ's resurrection, but actually the whole Bible is the history of God making a people for himself. Think about what this means for the work of Christ on the cross. There were countless believers in the Old Testament era. Hebrews 11 surveys a number of them, and they're presented as heroes of our faith, not of a different faith. The New Testament points back to the sacrifice of Christ on the cross; the Old Testament points *forward* to that same sacrifice. Jesus fulfilled the ceremonial and sacrificial requirements of the Old Testament law. They pointed to him. The Old Testament promises a Messiah to once-and-for-all do the work of which the ceremonies of the tabernacle and temple were only shadows. One could say, then, that their shadow was cast in the shape of the cross of Christ.

Ultimately believers in the Old Testament era were saved in the same way New Testament believers are saved: through faith in the work of Messiah. The difference is Old Testament believers believed in the promise that was *to be* fulfilled, while New Testament believers believe in the promise that *was* fulfilled. Same promise, just different sides of its fulfillment. The cross, therefore, stands above time, justifying believers no matter where they fall on the time line of history. That means the birth of the Church goes back to the beginning of belief. All true believers are united by faith. Some had a fuller revelation from God than others, but ultimately the *what* and *who* of their faith are the same. The Church was born because of the work of Christ on the cross and his resurrection. The effect of that work reaches forward to you and to me and to however many believers will live after our time but also back to the far-gone garden where Adam and Eve fell and were redeemed by our gracious God, who sacrificed an animal for them and clothed them with its skin. Then as now, God is a redeeming God, set on building his Church.

REFLECT AND DISCUSS

1. Describe your level of connection to a local church. Is your involvement feeding you and feeding others?

2. Do you think of church as a building or as a community of brothers and sisters who are united for eternity by faith in Christ? What needs to change in how you view the church?

3. Reading the list of beliefs found in the New Testament creeds, what were the surprises for you? Does the church you belong to deny any of these beliefs? If they do, or if anyone in your life does, how would you state the case for changing their minds?

4. The early church met regularly, fellowshipped, cared for one another, worshipped God passionately, and worked tirelessly to spread the gospel. Does this remind you of your present church? If so, thank your leaders. If not, consider and discuss what steps you can take to encourage change.

5. The Bible says Christ's followers shall be known by their fruits. If there are people in your life who profess to be Christians but do not seem to show the fruit of true faith, how might they be influencing you in negative ways? How are you influencing them in positive, careful ways that point toward the importance of true repentance and faith?

CHAPTER 6

MISSION TO THE WORLD

HAVE YOU EVER WONDERED what happened to the 12 disciples after Easter? Where they went, what they did, how they died? The book of Acts tells us about the birth of the Church and some activities of the Twelve, but it leaves unanswered many of the questions we might ask. To find answers, we have to look to traditions outside of the Bible. According to those traditions, most of the disciples were murdered due to their faith. Only John died of natural causes (at a very old age around AD 98). Not only were the other disciples martyred; some were killed in places surprisingly distant from Israel.

- Peter was crucified in Rome.
- James died by sword in Jerusalem.
- James Alphaeus was stoned in Jerusalem.
- Matthew was beheaded in Nabadah, Ethiopia.
- Bartholomew was crucified, flayed, and beheaded in Albinopolis, Armenia.
- Thomas was killed with a spear in India.
- Simon the Zealot was crucified in Britain.
- Matthias was stoned and beheaded in Jerusalem.
- Philip was crucified in Hieropolis, Turkey.
- Andrew and Jude were both crucified in Edessa, Greece.

Exact details differ among the historical sources, but tradition is unanimous that these were all martyred. Among Jesus's followers who weren't members of the 12 disciples, tradition tells us that Paul was martyred in Rome by Emperor Nero around the time of

AFTER EASTER

Peter's execution, and Jewish Roman historian Josephus reports that Jesus's brother James was finished off with a club to the head after being thrown from the highest point of the Jerusalem temple.

As interesting as it is to look into how and where the apostles died, the important question to answer is *why* they chose such a life. Why give up the comforts of home and social acceptance in order to travel all over the known world only to be beaten, imprisoned, starved, shipwrecked, persecuted, and eventually killed? Their mission didn't make them rich or powerful or bring them worldly advantage. They were despised as outcasts and troublemakers.

Think about Paul, for example. He had the advantage of being a well-educated Pharisee (Acts 22:3) and was set for a nice career. He was so committed to preserving tradition that he took the lead in persecuting anyone who followed the teachings of Jesus. Yet, as he traveled to Damascus intent on rounding up some Christians, something happened that caused him to believe in the very faith he was so passionately persecuting (Acts 9:1-19; 26:12-23; Galatians 1:11-24). He radically reoriented his life due to this conversion and spent the rest of his days preaching what he had once condemned. That he suffered for this preaching and proved willing to die for it shows that his conversion was a sure thing based on sure evidence. Simply put, there can be no reasonable doubt that Saul the unbeliever became Paul the believer because he encountered the one thing that could turn him around so radically: the risen Christ.

What the deaths of all the early martyrs have in common is that they weren't killed for *believing* Jesus as much as they were killed for *sharing* Jesus. They believed so strongly—on the basis of the resurrection—that they devoted their lives and resources to spreading the good news of Jesus throughout the world. The message of life was the cause of their death.

MISSION TO THE WORLD

Without the resurrection, Jesus's followers would have identified him as a teacher of morality who was utterly mistaken about his true identity. After all, claims of deity just don't mix well with execution on a Roman cross. And even though Jesus's moral teachings are extremely good, the truth is they're not really all that unique. Many ancient religions and law codes emphasized instructions that resemble Jesus's teachings. What makes Jesus unique is what he taught about *himself*. This aspect of his teaching, proven true by his resurrection, compelled the disciples to unlimited devotion.

Still, what is it that specifically made them drop their careers and hit the road in an endless quest to share everything they knew about Jesus? Seeing the risen Christ was enough to convince them of all he'd said, but it would've been easy to view that as a private belief rather than something to be shared with the world. Since Jesus had privately instructed the disciples during his ministry, it would've been understandable for them to think the "insider information" they'd been given was intended to remain their secret forever. They could further have rationalized their silence by saying God can save whomever he wants and doesn't need their help. Or they could've kept quiet because they didn't want to meddle in people's business. Religion is a touchy subject, after all. They also could've decided they didn't know enough or have the right gifts to share the message. There were all sorts of reasons they could've lain low and saved their skins. There had to be something that compelled them into foreign lands; that something was a direct command by Jesus.

After Jesus's resurrection, he appeared to many of his followers for the next 40 days. During this time he not only convinced them he'd risen from the dead; he also taught them further and prepared them for the important work they were to do. At his last appearance he tasked them with reaching the world:

AFTER EASTER

Then Jesus came near and said to them, "All
authority has been given to Me in heaven and
on earth. Go, therefore, and make disciples of all
nations, baptizing them in the name of the Father
and of the Son and of the Holy Spirit, teaching
them to observe everything I have commanded
you. And remember, I am with you always, to the
end of the age."

MATTHEW 28:18-20

This final instruction from Jesus is commonly called the Great
Commission. This is the answer to *why* the disciples would die for
their belief in Christ rather than cease spreading his message. This
is why they went to such extremes to make the gospel known in
parts of the world that hadn't heard. Proclaiming the good news
isn't optional, preferable, or recommended at our convenience. It's
imperative, a command of our Lord that applies not just to the
original disciples but to all disciples for all time. God has chosen to
spread the gospel primarily through the work of believers; he uses
his people to grow his people. Paul puts it this way:

But how can they call on Him they have not
believed in? And how can they believe without
hearing about Him? And how can they hear
without a preacher? And how can they preach
unless they are sent? As it is written: How
beautiful are the feet of those who announce the
gospel of good things! . . . So faith comes from

MISSION TO THE WORLD

what is heard, and what is heard comes through
the message about Christ. But I ask, "Did they not
hear?" Yes, they did:
Their voice has gone out to all the earth,
and their words to the ends
of the inhabited world.

ROMANS 10:14-15,17-18

Even though we're charged with the task of proclaiming the good news, it's not up to us to save anyone. Our job is to tell the truth in love as we find opportunity. Only through the work of the Holy Spirit can people come to faith, and we're his chosen vessels for giving people that opportunity.

Although the "great" in the Great Commission is the great news of the gospel, part of what makes the Great Commission so great is that it's great in scope. It's a message the whole world must hear, and therefore someone must take it there. It's a message for all cultures, all times, and all places. Jesus redeems people "from every tribe and language and people and nation" (Revelation 5:9). But to be redeemed, people must hear. And for people to hear requires believers who love them enough to go to the trouble of sharing Jesus with them. Often this sharing is unwelcome. Unbelievers commonly like being unbelievers. Our message is unwelcome or foolish to many of them, but we must risk rejection and share with them the only hope they can have for salvation.

Another way the Great Commission is great is in the great variety of ways it can be fulfilled. Jesus's command doesn't mean we all must leave everything behind and move to a foreign country; neither does it mean we must become itinerant evangelists, traveling nonstop as we share with everyone we meet. It might mean going on short-term mission trips, though. Travel to a disadvantaged place for a week or two. Serve hurting people so the gospel is lived out as well as proclaimed. Or it might mean sharing with all those God brings into your life. It can even be a combination of all of these things.

As long as we take the Great Commission seriously and are obedient when given opportunity to share, we'll be part of God's mission to the world. It's easy to think our acts of obedience are too insignificant to make a difference. After all (we tell ourselves), not everyone can be an Apostle Paul or a Billy Graham. But that kind of thinking is simply unbelief, and ultimately it accuses God of not being powerful enough to accomplish his will. That kind of thinking forgets that God was able to dramatically change the course of history and affect billions of lives starting with only a dozen simple men from a remote corner of a politically unimportant country at a time when there was no mass communication or easy transportation. If ever there were a mustard seed of faith that changed the world against all odds, this was it!

After Easter the early Christians not only had the good news and their encounters with the risen Christ; they also had a command to share what they knew with the world and a passionate desire to do it. That command isn't just for them; it's for us as well.

It's easy in our culture not to appreciate the great lengths our brothers and sisters in Christ have gone to in order to spread the good news. It's easy to think of reasons not to share. But if we take seriously the profound sacrifice of Christ and the extremes he went to in order to save us, we'll also repent of our fear and complacency and unbelief. We'll begin to understand why we *must* see ourselves as missionaries and take the gospel next door, down the street, to work, and to the world.

MISSION TO THE WORLD

REFLECT AND DISCUSS

1. Skeptical theories about Christian origins maintain that Jesus's disciples intentionally lied about Jesus's resurrection or else came to believe the resurrection on the basis of misperception or inflated expectations. How does the story of their deaths help us understand their belief in the resurrection? What difference does it make in our lives when we experience hardship for our faith?

2. Jesus's disciples were killed for *sharing* Jesus, not merely for believing in him. Any group of believers could protect themselves by choosing to keep their beliefs private. What does it say about the disciples' basis for belief that they shared despite the threats? Do you share the gospel despite potentially uncomfortable consequences?

3. How did you come to faith in Christ? Did it involve someone sharing the gospel with you? What approach did they take? What approach do you take when you share?

4. What excuses most tempt you to avoid telling others about your faith in Jesus? Describe how the Great Commission can help you overcome the temptations.

5. "A person's depth of confidence in the gospel is reflected in how often he shares the gospel with others." Do you agree or disagree with this statement. Why?

CHAPTER 7

ETERNAL DESTINIES

ADAM AND EVE WERE CREATED for durability. They were designed by God to exist forever and ever, and that design wasn't set aside when death invaded the world. Our death doesn't call into question *whether* we'll exist forever but *how* we'll exist forever. Because of sin our enduring existence is conditioned by a death penalty and two divergent eternities. Those who trust in Christ's redeeming work on their behalf will be raised up from death to exist forever with God in a state of incomprehensible abundance. Those left relying on their own works and false religions will be raised up to endure endless divine wrath.

Jesus's disciples knew this. They knew it from Scripture, and they knew it from him. They also had the privilege of experiencing aspects of Jesus's risen life, which means they eclipsed unassisted faith and speculative theories and got a firsthand taste of resurrection life. This plus the stark differences between the two eternal destinies awaiting us explains their willingness to expend their lives in the task of spreading gospel hope. Eternity is forever, after all, and souls are at stake. Possessing a sure solution, the disciples risked everything to share it with people.

Biblical revelations about what resurrected life and heaven will be like are minimal, but the things we've been shown are intriguing. After Easter, Jesus was recognizable, though with some qualifications. People who'd known him recognized him but were slow to do so for reasons unknown (Luke 24:16; John 20:15). He had a physical body that could be touched (Luke 24:39; John 20:27) and that could eat (Luke 24:42-43), but his body wasn't the same as his earthly body because it could pass through walls (John 20:19), didn't *need* to eat, and wouldn't grow old or sick. The same will be true for us:

> The dead will be raised incorruptible,
> and we will be changed.
> For this corruptible must be clothed
> with incorruptibility,
> and this mortal must be clothed
> with immortality.
> When this corruptible is clothed
> with incorruptibility,
> and this mortal is clothed
> with immortality. . .
>
> 1 CORINTHIANS 15:52-54

Everlasting life without suffering or evil is something we all desire, but that's secondary to the ultimate blessing: communion with God. Unrestrained access to God is our purpose and what we ultimately long for. This yearning makes our present world—no matter how good it can be at times—incomplete and unsatisfying.

> For we know that if our temporary, earthly
> dwelling is destroyed, we have a building from
> God, an eternal dwelling in the heavens, not
> made with hands. Indeed, we groan in this body,
> desiring to put on our dwelling from heaven,
> since, when we are clothed, we will not be found

> naked. Indeed, we groan while we are in this tent,
> burdened as we are, because we do not want
> to be unclothed but clothed, so that mortality
> may be swallowed up by life. And the One who
> prepared us for this very purpose is God, who
> gave us the Spirit as a down payment.
>
> 2 CORINTHIANS 5:1-5

Because Jesus died for our sins and because his righteousness was credited to us, Christians will stand before God blameless. He'll look on us but see the work of Christ. No shame, no guilt, no condemnation. In response, we'll cry out in praise and worship *forever*. The wonder of God will be inexhaustible. Paul calls it the "incomparable eternal weight of glory" (2 Corinthians 4:17).

Jesus calls heaven many things: paradise (Luke 23:43; Revelation 2:7), "My Father's house" (John 14:2), "the new Jerusalem, which comes down out of heaven" (Revelation 3:12). It's also called the "heavenly Jerusalem" (Hebrews 12:22) and the "Jerusalem above" (Galatians 4:26).

Heaven is more than a place; it's a state of being, where God's goodness is poured out fully and permanently. God's goodness can be seen in this world, but in heaven it will be seen fully. We will see God as he really is (1 John 3:2). The result is never-ending blessing and bliss. There will be no need of any kind, no dissatisfaction, and no distraction from enjoying God. Our obedience will be complete because we'll have changed natures. In our present life we're unable *not to* sin, but in the next life we'll be unable *to* sin. Jesus refers to this state as "the kingdom of heaven" (Matthew 25:1). God has been calling a people to this kingdom throughout history, and ultimately it's what he made us for:

ETERNAL DESTINIES

God's dwelling is with humanity,
and He will live with them.
They will be His people,
and God Himself will be with them
and be their God.
He will wipe away every tear from their eyes.
Death will no longer exist;
grief, crying, and pain will exist no longer,
because the previous things have passed away.

REVELATION 21:3-4

Eternal life is life truly *alive*, life without the allure of sin or the curse of death marring our experience of the world. It's eternal not only in quantity but in quality. Peter puts it this way:

According to His great mercy, He has given
us a new birth into a living hope through the
resurrection of Jesus Christ from the dead
and into an inheritance that is imperishable,
uncorrupted, and unfading, kept in heaven for
you. You are being protected by God's power
through faith for a salvation that is ready to be
revealed in the last time.

1 PETER 1:3-5

Not everyone will be raised to live eternally in heaven. The hard truth is that the road leading there is narrow and few find it. A broader path, filled with the many rather than the few, runs spiraling down into final despair. No blessing from God will ever visit that place. There will be nothing to live for in that darkness, no good to receive, no good to do, no hope for anything to improve. Ever.

As bad as that sounds, it gets worse. Inhabitants of hell aren't merely without hope; they're subjected to eternal punishment as God pours out his wrath against evil. Sometimes we think of hell as the place where God is absent, but there's no such place in the universe. God is everywhere. Theologians call this omnipresence (omni = all). In fact, hell couldn't be hell unless God is there to dole out his judgment. A Godless hell would leave unbelievers in exactly the state they've desired: free from God's authority. Instead of freedom from God, the damned will be confronted unendingly by God. Paul writes:

> For God's wrath is revealed from heaven against all godlessness and unrighteousness of people who by their unrighteousness suppress the truth, since what can be known about God is evident among them, because God has shown it to them. For His invisible attributes, that is, His eternal power and divine nature, have been clearly seen since the creation of the world, being understood through what He has made. As a result, people are without excuse. For though they knew God, they did not glorify Him as God or show gratitude. Instead, their thinking became nonsense, and their senseless minds were darkened. Claiming to be wise, they became fools

ETERNAL DESTINIES

and exchanged the glory of the immortal God for
images resembling mortal man, birds, four-footed
animals, and reptiles.
Therefore God delivered them over in the
cravings of their hearts to sexual impurity, so that
their bodies were degraded among themselves.
They exchanged the truth of God for a lie, and
worshiped and served something created instead
of the Creator, who is praised forever. Amen. . . .
Although they know full well God's just
sentence—that those who practice such things
deserve to die—they not only do them, but even
applaud others who practice them.

ROMANS 1:18-25,32

Hell is such a hard teaching that many have insisted a loving God just wouldn't do what the preachers say he'll do. Punish someone forever simply for not believing in him? No way. This argument has a strong emotional pull, but it misrepresents what happens in hell and ignores the clear biblical witness. People aren't sent to hell for unbelief. Rather, everyone will be judged by works, and the standard that must be met is perfection (Revelation 20:11-15). Either we're judged by the works of Christ, or we're judged by our own works. If we're never redeemed through faith in Christ, we'll face God with nothing to offer but our own works. Those inevitably fail to meet God's standard. It's also important to note that no one in hell will be tortured. Torture is a barbaric tactic in which pain is inflicted not for punishment but for pleasure or to achieve some intended outcome, such as the disclosure of information. The damned in hell aren't tortured; they're justly punished.

AFTER EASTER

The Bible describes hell as the place where the wicked are sent (Psalm 31:17). It's said to be deep (Job 11:8), equipped with gates (Job 17:16); it is described as a prison (1 Peter 3:19) and can be locked (Revelation 1:18). It's a place of profound suffering (Matthew 8:12; 25:30), a fiery furnace (Matthew 13:42) of flames (Luke 16:24) and a lake of fire (Revelation 20:14-15), and yet it is also described as outer darkness (Matthew 22:13). It's a place where the inhabitants receive "wrath and indignation" (Romans 2:8). Three things are clear from these descriptions: hell is real, it's terrible, and evil is quarantined there so it won't taint the rest of the future new creation.

The imagery is frightening, but maybe consignment to hell is only temporary. Some have said so, reasoning that sins committed in a finite lifetime don't merit eternal punishment. The lost will eventually be annihilated, they say, and hell itself will be doused once God has satisfied his wrath.

This theory runs afoul of at least two important points. First, sinners may be finite, but their sins are not. Sin, *any* sin, is an assault on the holy nature of infinite God and thus the offense is infinite. Sinners are either pardoned by substitute righteousness (Christ's, given to believers through faith), or else they stand eternally in need of punishment.

Second, Jesus taught that hell is eternal. While talking about the false claims of the Pharisees, he said, "They will go away into eternal punishment, but the righteous into eternal life" (Matthew 25:46). Similarly in the Old Testament the prophet Daniel says some people will receive eternal life and others eternal contempt.

In summary, there's no escaping the biblical teaching on hell and no explaining it away to soften the blow. Hell is a terrible and certain fact. It awaits all who die in their sins. The apostles knew this and felt the urgency of it. It motivated them to share the gospel at all costs, and our response should be the same.

ETERNAL DESTINIES

✝

In the end even those who reject God will bow their knee to him.

For this reason God highly exalted Him
and gave Him the name
that is above every name,
so that at the name of Jesus
every knee will bow—
of those who are in heaven and on earth
and under the earth—
and every tongue should confess
that Jesus Christ is Lord,
to the glory of God the Father.

PHILIPPIANS 2:9-11

The question for each of us is, will we bow the knee willingly, while we can still find forgiveness, or will we bow only under obligation when it's too late? Why wait any longer? Christian hope is grounded in the well-established fact of Jesus's resurrection. After Easter we aren't asked to have blind faith. We *know* that Jesus is alive. We *know* that he was telling the truth about himself, the world, and his work as Savior. After Easter, we can *know*.

REFLECT AND DISCUSS

1. What do you believe about life after death? What new thoughts do you have after reading this chapter? Briefly describe how you would summarize the biblical view if someone asked you to do so.

2. When you think of heaven, do you think primarily of being reunited with lost loved ones and experiencing the grandeur of it all, or do you primarily think of being in God's presence and enjoying him forever? Which of those values best matches the biblical emphasis on heaven? Why?

3. When you read that we will worship God forever in heaven, what comes to mind? The biblical view of worship is more expansive than just singing and praying. What are some ways you can imagine you will worship God in heaven? How will your worship in heaven differ from your worship on earth?

4. Jesus spoke about hell more often than he did about heaven. But many today choose not to believe in hell, rejecting a core biblical teaching. Why do you think people pick and choose what to accept from the Bible? If the Bible is from God, as it claims to be, is it legitimate to pick and choose?

5. If you accept hell as real, what considerations could possibly keep you from sharing the gospel with unbelievers who are doomed to go there unless they repent and accept Christ? Who are the people in your life who need to hear about the good news of Jesus Christ?

JOHN

1 In the beginning was the Word,[A]
and the Word was with God,
and the Word was God.
² He was with God in the beginning.
³ All things were created
    through Him,
and apart from Him not one thing
    was created
that has been created.
⁴ Life was in Him,[B]
and that life was the light of men.
⁵ That light shines in the darkness,
yet the darkness did not overcome[C] it.

⁶ There was a man named John
who was sent from God.
⁷ He came as a witness
to testify about the light,
so that all might believe through him.[D]
⁸ He was not the light,
but he came to testify about the light.
⁹ The true light, who gives light
    to everyone,
was coming into the world.[E]

¹⁰ He was in the world,
and the world was created
    through Him,
yet the world did not
    recognize Him.
¹¹ He came to His own,[F]
and His own people[F]
    did not receive Him.
¹² But to all who did receive Him,
He gave them the right to be[G]
    children of God,
to those who believe in His name,
¹³ who were born,
not of blood,[H]
or of the will of the flesh,
or of the will of man,[I]
but of God.

¹⁴ The Word became flesh[J]
and took up residence[K] among us.
We observed His glory,
the glory as the One and Only Son[L]
    from the Father,
full of grace and truth.
¹⁵ (John testified concerning Him
    and exclaimed,
"This was the One of whom I said,
'The One coming after me
    has surpassed me,
because He existed before me.'")
¹⁶ Indeed, we have all received grace
    after grace
from His fullness,
¹⁷ for the law was given through Moses,
grace and truth came
    through Jesus Christ.
¹⁸ No one has ever seen God.[M]
The One and Only Son[N]—
the One who is at the Father's side[O]—
He has revealed Him.

¹⁹ This is John's testimony when the Jews from Jerusalem sent priests and Levites to ask him, "Who are you?"
²⁰ He did not refuse to answer, but he declared: "I am not the Messiah."
²¹ "What then?" they asked him. "Are you Elijah?"

"I am not," he said.

"Are you the Prophet?"[P]

"No," he answered.

²² "Who are you, then?" they asked. "We need to give an answer to those who sent us. What can you tell us about yourself?"
²³ He said, "I am a **voice of one crying out in the wilderness: Make straight the way of the Lord**[Q]—just as Isaiah the prophet said."
²⁴ Now they had been sent from the Pharisees. ²⁵ So they asked him, "Why then do you baptize if you aren't the Messiah, or Elijah, or the Prophet?"

²⁶"I baptize with^A water," John answered them. "Someone stands among you, but you don't know Him. ²⁷He is the One coming after me,^B whose sandal strap I'm not worthy to untie."

²⁸All this happened in Bethany^C across the Jordan,^D where John was baptizing.

²⁹The next day John saw Jesus coming toward him and said, "Here is the Lamb of God, who takes away the sin of the world! ³⁰This is the One I told you about: 'After me comes a man who has surpassed me, because He existed before me.' ³¹I didn't know Him, but I came baptizing with^A water so He might be revealed to Israel."

³²And John testified, "I watched the Spirit descending from heaven like a dove, and He rested on Him. ³³I didn't know Him, but He^E who sent me to baptize with^A water told me, 'The One you see the Spirit descending and resting on—He is the One who baptizes with^A the Holy Spirit.' ³⁴I have seen and testified that He is the Son of God!"^F

³⁵Again the next day, John was standing with two of his disciples. ³⁶When he saw Jesus passing by, he said, "Look! The Lamb of God!"

³⁷The two disciples heard him say this and followed Jesus. ³⁸When Jesus turned and noticed them following Him, He asked them, "What are you looking for?"

They said to Him, "Rabbi" (which means "Teacher"), "where are You staying?"

³⁹"Come and you'll see," He replied. So they went and saw where He was staying, and they stayed with Him that day. It was about 10 in the morning.^G

⁴⁰Andrew, Simon Peter's brother, was one of the two who heard John and followed Him. ⁴¹He first found his own brother Simon and told him, "We have found the Messiah!"^H (which means "Anointed One"), ⁴²and he brought Simon to Jesus.

When Jesus saw him, He said, "You are Simon, son of John.^I You will be called Cephas" (which means "Rock").

⁴³The next day He^J decided to leave for Galilee. Jesus found Philip and told him, "Follow Me!"

⁴⁴Now Philip was from Bethsaida, the hometown of Andrew and Peter. ⁴⁵Philip found Nathanael^K and told him, "We have found the One Moses wrote about in the Law (and so did the prophets): Jesus the son of Joseph, from Nazareth!"

⁴⁶"Can anything good come out of Nazareth?" Nathanael asked him.

"Come and see," Philip answered.

⁴⁷Then Jesus saw Nathanael coming toward Him and said about him, "Here is a true Israelite; no deceit is in him."

⁴⁸"How do you know me?" Nathanael asked.

"Before Philip called you, when you were under the fig tree, I saw you," Jesus answered.

⁴⁹"Rabbi," Nathanael replied, "You are the Son of God! You are the King of Israel!"

⁵⁰Jesus responded to him, "Do you believe only because I told you I saw you under the fig tree? You^L will see greater things than this." ⁵¹Then He said, "I assure you: You^M will see heaven opened and the angels of God ascending and descending on the Son of Man."

2 On the third day a wedding took place in Cana of Galilee. Jesus' mother was there, and ²Jesus and His disciples were invited to the wedding as well. ³When the wine ran out, Jesus' mother told Him, "They don't have any wine."

⁴"What has this concern of yours to do with Me,^N woman?" Jesus asked. "My hour^O has not yet come."

⁵"Do whatever He tells you," His mother told the servants.

⁶Now six stone water jars had been set there for Jewish purification. Each contained 20 or 30 gallons.^P

⁷"Fill the jars with water," Jesus told them. So they filled them to the brim. ⁸Then He said to them, "Now draw some out and take it to the chief servant."^Q And they did.

^A1:26,31,33 Or *in*   ^B1:27 Other mss add *who came before me*   ^C1:28 Other mss read *in Bethabara*   ^D1:28 Another Bethany, near Jerusalem, was the home of Lazarus, Martha, and Mary; Jn 11:1.   ^E1:33 *He* refers to God the Father, who gave John a sign to help him identify the Messiah. Vv. 32-34 indicate that John did not know that Jesus was the Messiah until the Spirit descended upon Him at His baptism.   ^F1:34 Other mss read *is the Chosen One of God*   ^G1:39 Lit *about the tenth hour*. Various methods of reckoning time were used in the ancient world. John probably used a different method from the other 3 Gospels. If John used the same method of time reckoning as the other 3 Gospels, the translation would be: *It was about four in the afternoon.*   ^H1:41 In the NT, the word Messiah translates the Gk word *Christos* ["Anointed One"], except here and in Jn 4:25 where it translates *Messias*.   ^I1:42 Other mss read *Simon, son of Jonah*   ^J1:43 Or *he*, referring either to Simon Peter [vv. 41-42] or Andrew [vv. 40-41]   ^K1:45 Probably the Bartholomew of the other Gospels and Acts   ^L1:50 In Gk, the word you is sg and refers to Nathanael.   ^M1:51 In Gk, the word you is pl and refers to Nathanael and the other disciples.   ^N2:4 Or *You and I see things differently*; lit *What to Me and to you*; Mt 8:29; Mk 1:24; 5:7; Lk 8:28   ^O2:4 The time of His sacrificial death and exaltation; Jn 7:30; 8:20; 12:23,27; 13:1; 17:1   ^P2:6 Lit *2 or 3 measures*   ^Q2:8 Lit *ruler of the table*; perhaps *master of the feast*, or *headwaiter*

⁹When the chief servant tasted the water (after it had become wine), he did not know where it came from—though the servants who had drawn the water knew. He called the groom ¹⁰and told him, "Everyone sets out the fine wine first, then, after people have drunk freely, the inferior. But you have kept the fine wine until now."

¹¹Jesus performed this first sign^A in Cana of Galilee. He displayed His glory, and His disciples believed in Him.

¹²After this, He went down to Capernaum, together with His mother, His brothers, and His disciples, and they stayed there only a few days.

¹³The Jewish Passover was near, so Jesus went up to Jerusalem. ¹⁴In the temple complex He found people selling oxen, sheep, and doves, and He also found the money changers sitting there. ¹⁵After making a whip out of cords, He drove everyone out of the temple complex with their sheep and oxen. He also poured out the money changers' coins and overturned the tables. ¹⁶He told those who were selling doves, "Get these things out of here! Stop turning My Father's house into a marketplace!"^B

¹⁷And His disciples remembered that it is written: **Zeal for Your house will consume Me.**^C

¹⁸So the Jews replied to Him, "What sign of authority will You show us for doing these things?"

¹⁹Jesus answered, "Destroy this sanctuary, and I will raise it up in three days."

²⁰Therefore the Jews said, "This sanctuary took 46 years to build, and will You raise it up in three days?"

²¹But He was speaking about the sanctuary of His body. ²²So when He was raised from the dead, His disciples remembered that He had said this. And they believed the Scripture and the statement Jesus had made.

²³While He was in Jerusalem at the Passover Festival, many trusted in His name when they saw the signs He was doing. ²⁴Jesus, however, would not entrust Himself to them, since He knew them all ²⁵and because He did not need

anyone to testify about man; for He Himself knew what was in man.

3 There was a man from the Pharisees named Nicodemus, a ruler of the Jews. ²This man came to Him at night and said, "Rabbi, we know that You have come from God as a teacher, for no one could perform these signs You do unless God were with him."

³Jesus replied, "I assure you: Unless someone is born again,^D he cannot see the kingdom of God."

⁴"But how can anyone be born when he is old?" Nicodemus asked Him. "Can he enter his mother's womb a second time and be born?"

⁵Jesus answered, "I assure you: Unless someone is born of water and the Spirit,^E he cannot enter the kingdom of God. ⁶Whatever is born of the flesh is flesh, and whatever is born of the Spirit is spirit. ⁷Do not be amazed that I told you that you^F must be born again. ⁸The wind^G blows where it pleases, and you hear its sound, but you don't know where it comes from or where it is going. So it is with everyone born of the Spirit."

⁹"How can these things be?" asked Nicodemus.

¹⁰"Are you a teacher^H of Israel and don't know these things?" Jesus replied. ¹¹"I assure you: We speak what We know and We testify to what We have seen, but you^I do not accept Our testimony.^J ¹²If I have told you about things that happen on earth and you don't believe, how will you believe if I tell you about things of heaven? ¹³No one has ascended into heaven except the One who descended from heaven—the Son of Man.^K ¹⁴Just as Moses lifted up the snake in the wilderness, so the Son of Man must be lifted up, ¹⁵so that everyone who believes in Him will^L have eternal life.

¹⁶"For God loved the world in this way:^M He gave His One and Only Son, so that everyone who believes in Him will not perish but have eternal life. ¹⁷For God did not send His Son into the world that He might condemn the world, but that the world might be saved through Him. ¹⁸Anyone who believes in Him is not condemned, but anyone who does not

^A 2:11 Lit *this beginning of the signs*; Jn 4:54; 20:30. Seven miraculous signs occur in John's Gospel and are so noted in the headings.
^B 2:16 Lit *a house of business*   ^C 2:17 Ps 69:9   ^D 3:3 The same Gk word can mean again or from above (also in v. 7).   ^E 3:5 Or *spirit*, or *wind*; the Gk word *pneuma* can mean *wind*, *spirit*, or *Spirit*, each of which occurs in this context.   ^F 3:7 The pronoun is pl in Gk.   ^G 3:8 The Gk word *pneuma* can mean wind, spirit, or Spirit, each of which occurs in this context.   ^H 3:10 Or *the teacher*   ^I 3:11 In Gk, the word you is pl here and throughout v. 12.   ^J 3:11 The pronouns we and our refer to Jesus and His authority to speak for the Father.   ^K 3:13 Other mss add *who is in heaven*   ^L 3:15 Other mss add *not perish, but*   ^M 3:16 The Gk word *houtos*, commonly translated in Jn 3:16 as "so" or "so much" occurs over 200 times in the NT. Almost without exception it is an adverb of manner, not degree (for example, see Mt 1:18). It only means "so much" when modifying an adjective (see Gl 3:3; Rv 16:18). Manner seems primarily in view in Jn 3:16, which explains the HCSB's rendering.

believe is already condemned, because he has not believed in the name of the One and Only Son of God.

¹⁹"This, then, is the judgment: The light has come into the world, and people loved darkness rather than the light because their deeds were evil. ²⁰For everyone who practices wicked things hates the light and avoids it,ᴬ so that his deeds may not be exposed. ²¹But anyone who lives byᴮ the truth comes to the light, so that his works may be shown to be accomplished by God."ᶜ

²²After this, Jesus and His disciples went to the Judean countryside, where He spent time with them and baptized. ²³John also was baptizing in Aenon near Salim, because there was plenty of water there. People were coming and being baptized, ²⁴since John had not yet been thrown into prison.

²⁵Then a dispute arose between John's disciples and a Jewᴰ about purification. ²⁶So they came to John and told him, "Rabbi, the One you testified about, and who was with you across the Jordan, is baptizing—and everyone is flocking to Him."

²⁷John responded, "No one can receive a single thing unless it's given to him from heaven. ²⁸You yourselves can testify that I said, 'I am not the Messiah, but I've been sent ahead of Him.' ²⁹He who has the bride is the groom. But the groom's friend, who stands by and listens for him, rejoices greatlyᴱ at the groom's voice. So this joy of mine is complete. ³⁰He must increase, but I must decrease."

³¹The One who comes from above is above all. The one who is from the earth is earthly and speaks in earthly terms.ᶠ The One who comes from heaven is above all. ³²He testifies to what He has seen and heard, yet no one accepts His testimony. ³³The one who has accepted His testimony has affirmed that God is true. ³⁴For God sent Him, and He speaks God's words, since Heᴳ gives the Spirit without measure. ³⁵The Father loves the Son and has given all things into His hands. ³⁶The one who believes in the Son has eternal life, but the one who refuses to believe in the Son will not see life; instead, the wrath of God remains on him.

4 When Jesusᴴ knew that the Pharisees heard He was making and baptizing more disciples than John ²(though Jesus Himself was not baptizing, but His disciples were), ³He left Judea and went again to Galilee. ⁴He had to travel through Samaria, ⁵so He came to a town of Samaria called Sychar near the propertyᴵ that Jacob had given his son Joseph. ⁶Jacob's well was there, and Jesus, worn out from His journey, sat down at the well. It was about six in the evening.ᴶ

⁷A woman of Samaria came to draw water.

"Give Me a drink," Jesus said to her, ⁸for His disciples had gone into town to buy food.

⁹"How is it that You, a Jew, ask for a drink from me, a Samaritan woman?" she asked Him. For Jews do not associate withᴷ Samaritans.ᴸ

¹⁰Jesus answered, "If you knew the gift of God, and who is saying to you, 'Give Me a drink,' you would ask Him, and He would give you living water."

¹¹"Sir," said the woman, "You don't even have a bucket, and the well is deep. So where do You get this 'living water'? ¹²You aren't greater than our father Jacob, are You? He gave us the well and drank from it himself, as did his sons and livestock."

¹³Jesus said, "Everyone who drinks from this water will get thirsty again. ¹⁴But whoever drinks from the water that I will give him will never get thirsty again—ever! In fact, the water I will give him will become a wellᴹ of water springing up within him for eternal life."

¹⁵"Sir," the woman said to Him, "give me this water so I won't get thirsty and come here to draw water."

¹⁶"Go call your husband," He told her, "and come back here."

¹⁷"I don't have a husband," she answered.

"You have correctly said, 'I don't have a husband,'" Jesus said. ¹⁸"For you've had five husbands, and the man you now have is not your husband. What you have said is true."

¹⁹"Sir," the woman replied, "I see that You are a prophet. ²⁰Our fathers worshiped on this mountain,ᴺ yet you Jews say that the place to worship is in Jerusalem."

ᴬ3:20 Lit *and does not come to the light*   ᴮ3:21 Lit *who does*   ᶜ3:21 It is possible that Jesus' words end at v. 15. Ancient Gk did not have quotation marks.   ᴰ3:25 Other mss read *and the Jews*   ᴱ3:29 Lit *with joy rejoices*   ᶠ3:31 Or *of earthly things*   ᴳ3:34 Other mss read *since God*   ᴴ4:1 Other mss read *the Lord*   ᴵ4:5 Lit *piece of land*   ᴶ4:6 Lit *the sixth hour*; see note at Jn 1:39; an alt time reckoning would be *noon*   ᴷ4:9 Or *do not share vessels with*   ᴸ4:9 Other mss omit *For Jews do not associate with Samaritans.*   ᴹ4:14 Or *spring*   ᴺ4:20 Mount Gerizim, where there had been a Samaritan temple that rivaled Jerusalem's

²¹ Jesus told her, "Believe Me, woman, an hour is coming when you will worship the Father neither on this mountain nor in Jerusalem. ²² You Samaritans^A worship what you do not know. We worship what we do know, because salvation is from the Jews. ²³ But an hour is coming, and is now here, when the true worshipers will worship the Father in spirit and truth. Yes, the Father wants such people to worship Him. ²⁴ God is spirit, and those who worship Him must worship in spirit and truth."

²⁵ The woman said to Him, "I know that Messiah^B is coming" (who is called Christ). "When He comes, He will explain everything to us."

²⁶ "I am He," Jesus told her, "the One speaking to you."

²⁷ Just then His disciples arrived, and they were amazed that He was talking with a woman. Yet no one said, "What do You want?" or "Why are You talking with her?"

²⁸ Then the woman left her water jar, went into town, and told the men, ²⁹ "Come, see a man who told me everything I ever did! Could this be the Messiah?" ³⁰ They left the town and made their way to Him.

³¹ In the meantime the disciples kept urging Him, "Rabbi, eat something."

³² But He said, "I have food to eat that you don't know about."

³³ The disciples said to one another, "Could someone have brought Him something to eat?"

³⁴ "My food is to do the will of Him who sent Me and to finish His work," Jesus told them. ³⁵ "Don't you say, 'There are still four more months, then comes the harvest'? Listen to what I'm telling you: Open^C your eyes and look at the fields, for they are ready^D for harvest. ³⁶ The reaper is already receiving pay and gathering fruit for eternal life, so the sower and reaper can rejoice together. ³⁷ For in this case the saying is true: 'One sows and another reaps.' ³⁸ I sent you to reap what you didn't labor for; others have labored, and you have benefited from^E their labor."

³⁹ Now many Samaritans from that town believed in Him because of what the woman said^F when she testified, "He told me everything I ever did." ⁴⁰ Therefore, when the Samaritans came to Him, they asked Him to stay with them, and He stayed there two days. ⁴¹ Many more believed because of what He said.^G ⁴² And they told the woman, "We no longer believe because of what you said, for we have heard for ourselves and know that this really is the Savior of the world."^H

⁴³ After two days He left there for Galilee. ⁴⁴ Jesus Himself testified that a prophet has no honor in his own country. ⁴⁵ When they entered Galilee, the Galileans welcomed Him because they had seen everything He did in Jerusalem during the festival. For they also had gone to the festival.

⁴⁶ Then He went again to Cana of Galilee, where He had turned the water into wine. There was a certain royal official whose son was ill at Capernaum. ⁴⁷ When this man heard that Jesus had come from Judea into Galilee, he went to Him and pleaded with Him to come down and heal his son, for he was about to die.

⁴⁸ Jesus told him, "Unless you people see signs and wonders, you will not believe."

⁴⁹ "Sir," the official said to Him, "come down before my boy dies!"

⁵⁰ "Go," Jesus told him, "your son will live." The man believed what^I Jesus said to him and departed.

⁵¹ While he was still going down, his slaves met him saying that his boy was alive. ⁵² He asked them at what time he got better. "Yesterday at seven in the morning^J the fever left him," they answered. ⁵³ The father realized this was the very hour at which Jesus had told him, "Your son will live." Then he himself believed, along with his whole household.

⁵⁴ This, therefore, was the second sign Jesus performed after He came from Judea to Galilee.

5 After this, a Jewish festival took place, and Jesus went up to Jerusalem. ² By the Sheep Gate in Jerusalem there is a pool, called Bethesda^K in Hebrew, which has five colonnades.^L ³ Within these lay a large number of the sick—blind, lame, and paralyzed [—waiting for the moving of the water, ⁴ because an angel would go down into the pool from time to time and stir up the water. Then the first one who got in after the water was stirred up recovered from whatever ailment he had].^M

⁵ One man was there who had been sick for 38 years. ⁶ When Jesus saw him lying there and

---

^A**4:22** *Samaritans* is implied since the Gk verb and pronoun are pl.   ^B**4:25** In the NT, the word Messiah translates the Gk word *Christos* ("Anointed One"), except here and in Jn 1:41 where it translates *Messias*.   ^C**4:35** Lit *Raise*   ^D**4:35** Lit *white*   ^E**4:38** Lit *you have entered into*   ^F**4:39** Lit *because of the woman's word*   ^G**4:41** Lit *because of His word*   ^H**4:42** Other mss add *the Messiah*   ^I**4:50** Lit *the word*   ^J**4:52** Or *seven in the evening*; lit *at the seventh hour*; see note at Jn 1:39; an alt time reckoning would be *at one in the afternoon*   ^K**5:2** Other mss read *Bethzatha*; other mss read *Bethsaida*   ^L**5:2** Rows of columns supporting a roof   ^M**5:3-4** Other mss omit bracketed text

knew he had already been there a long time, He said to him, "Do you want to get well?"

[7] "Sir," the sick man answered, "I don't have a man to put me into the pool when the water is stirred up, but while I'm coming, someone goes down ahead of me."

[8] "Get up," Jesus told him, "pick up your mat and walk!" [9] Instantly the man got well, picked up his mat, and started to walk.

Now that day was the Sabbath, [10] so the Jews said to the man who had been healed, "This is the Sabbath! It's illegal for you to pick up your mat."

[11] He replied, "The man who made me well told me, 'Pick up your mat and walk.'"

[12] "Who is this man who told you, 'Pick up your mat and walk'?" they asked. [13] But the man who was cured did not know who it was, because Jesus had slipped away into the crowd that was there.[A]

[14] After this, Jesus found him in the temple complex and said to him, "See, you are well. Do not sin anymore, so that something worse doesn't happen to you." [15] The man went and reported to the Jews that it was Jesus who had made him well.

[16] Therefore, the Jews began persecuting Jesus[B] because He was doing these things on the Sabbath. [17] But Jesus responded to them, "My Father is still working, and I am working also." [18] This is why the Jews began trying all the more to kill Him: Not only was He breaking the Sabbath, but He was even calling God His own Father, making Himself equal with God.

[19] Then Jesus replied, "I assure you: The Son is not able to do anything on His own, but only what He sees the Father doing. For whatever the Father[C] does, the Son also does these things in the same way. [20] For the Father loves the Son and shows Him everything He is doing, and He will show Him greater works than these so that you will be amazed. [21] And just as the Father raises the dead and gives them life, so the Son also gives life to anyone He wants to. [22] The Father, in fact, judges no one but has given all judgment to the Son, [23] so that all people will honor the Son just as they honor the Father. Anyone who does not honor the Son does not honor the Father who sent Him.

[24] "I assure you: Anyone who hears My word and believes Him who sent Me has eternal life and will not come under judgment but has passed from death to life.

[25] "I assure you: An hour is coming, and is now here, when the dead will hear the voice of the Son of God, and those who hear will live. [26] For just as the Father has life in Himself, so also He has granted to the Son to have life in Himself. [27] And He has granted Him the right to pass judgment, because He is the Son of Man. [28] Do not be amazed at this, because a time is coming when all who are in the graves will hear His voice [29] and come out—those who have done good things, to the resurrection of life, but those who have done wicked things, to the resurrection of judgment.

[30] "I can do nothing on My own. I judge only as I hear, and My judgment is righteous, because I do not seek My own will, but the will of Him who sent Me.

[31] "If I testify about Myself, My testimony is not valid.[D] [32] There is Another who testifies about Me, and I know that the testimony He gives about Me is valid.[E] [33] You have sent messengers to John, and he has testified to the truth. [34] I don't receive man's testimony, but I say these things so that you may be saved. [35] John[F] was a burning and shining lamp, and for a time you were willing to enjoy his light.

[36] "But I have a greater testimony than John's because of the works that the Father has given Me to accomplish. These very works I am doing testify about Me that the Father has sent Me. [37] The Father who sent Me has Himself testified about Me. You have not heard His voice at any time, and you haven't seen His form. [38] You don't have His word living in you, because you don't believe the One He sent. [39] You pore over[G] the Scriptures because you think you have eternal life in them, yet they testify about Me. [40] And you are not willing to come to Me so that you may have life.

[41] "I do not accept glory from men, [42] but I know you—that you have no love for God within you. [43] I have come in My Father's name, yet you don't accept Me. If someone else comes in his own name, you will accept him. [44] How can you believe? While accepting glory from one another, you don't seek the glory that comes from the only God. [45] Do not think that I will accuse you to the Father. Your accuser is Moses, on whom you have set your hope. [46] For if you believed Moses, you would

believe Me, because he wrote about Me. ⁴⁷But if you don't believe his writings, how will you believe My words?"

6 After this, Jesus crossed the Sea of Galilee (or Tiberias). ²And a huge crowd was following Him because they saw the signs that He was performing by healing the sick. ³So Jesus went up a mountain and sat down there with His disciples.

⁴Now the Passover, a Jewish festival, was near. ⁵Therefore, when Jesus looked up and noticed a huge crowd coming toward Him, He asked Philip, "Where will we buy bread so these people can eat?" ⁶He asked this to test him, for He Himself knew what He was going to do.

⁷Philip answered, "Two hundred denarii worth of bread wouldn't be enough for each of them to have a little."

⁸One of His disciples, Andrew, Simon Peter's brother, said to Him, ⁹"There's a boy here who has five barley loaves and two fish—but what are they for so many?"

¹⁰Then Jesus said, "Have the people sit down."

There was plenty of grass in that place, so they sat down. The men numbered about 5,000. ¹¹Then Jesus took the loaves, and after giving thanks He distributed them to those who were seated—so also with the fish, as much as they wanted.

¹²When they were full, He told His disciples, "Collect the leftovers so that nothing is wasted." ¹³So they collected them and filled 12 baskets with the pieces from the five barley loaves that were left over by those who had eaten.

¹⁴When the people saw the sign^A He had done, they said, "This really is the Prophet who was to come into the world!" ¹⁵Therefore, when Jesus knew that they were about to come and take Him by force to make Him king, He withdrew again^B to the mountain by Himself.

¹⁶When evening came, His disciples went down to the sea, ¹⁷got into a boat, and started across the sea to Capernaum. Darkness had already set in, but Jesus had not yet come to them. ¹⁸Then a high wind arose, and the sea began to churn. ¹⁹After they had rowed about three or four miles,^C they saw Jesus walking on the sea. He was coming near the boat, and they were afraid.

²⁰But He said to them, "It is I.^D Don't be afraid!" ²¹Then they were willing to take Him on board, and at once the boat was at the shore where they were heading.

²²The next day, the crowd that had stayed on the other side of the sea knew there had been only one boat.^E They also knew that Jesus had not boarded the boat with His disciples, but that His disciples had gone off alone. ²³Some boats from Tiberias came near the place where they ate the bread after the Lord gave thanks. ²⁴When the crowd saw that neither Jesus nor His disciples were there, they got into the boats and went to Capernaum looking for Jesus.

²⁵When they found Him on the other side of the sea, they said to Him, "Rabbi, when did You get here?"

²⁶Jesus answered, "I assure you: You are looking for Me, not because you saw^F the signs, but because you ate the loaves and were filled. ²⁷Don't work for the food that perishes but for the food that lasts for eternal life, which the Son of Man will give you, because God the Father has set His seal of approval on Him."

²⁸"What can we do to perform the works of God?" they asked.

²⁹Jesus replied, "This is the work of God—that you believe in the One He has sent."

³⁰"What sign then are You going to do so we may see and believe You?" they asked. "What are You going to perform? ³¹Our fathers ate the manna in the wilderness, just as it is written: **He gave them bread from heaven to eat.**"^G,H

³²Jesus said to them, "I assure you: Moses didn't give you the bread from heaven, but My Father gives you the real bread from heaven. ³³For the bread of God is the One who comes down from heaven and gives life to the world."

³⁴Then they said, "Sir, give us this bread always!"

³⁵"I am the bread of life," Jesus told them. "No one who comes to Me will ever be hungry, and no one who believes in Me will ever be thirsty again. ³⁶But as I told you, you've seen Me,^I and yet you do not believe. ³⁷Everyone the Father gives Me will come to Me, and the one who comes to Me I will never cast out. ³⁸For I have come down from heaven, not to do My will, but the will of Him who sent Me. ³⁹This is the will of Him who sent Me: that I should lose

^A6:14 Other mss read *signs*   ^B6:15 A previous withdrawal is mentioned in Mk 6:31-32, an event that occurred just before the feeding of the 5,000.   ^C6:19 Lit *25 or 30 stadia*; 1 *stadion* = 600 feet   ^D6:20 Lit *I am*   ^E6:22 Other mss add *into which His disciples had entered*   ^F6:26 Or *perceived*   ^G6:31 Bread miraculously provided by God for the Israelites   ^H6:31 Ex 16:4; Ps 78:24   ^I6:36 Other mss omit *Me*

none of those He has given Me but should raise them up on the last day. [40]For this is the will of My Father: that everyone who sees the Son and believes in Him may have eternal life, and I will raise him up on the last day."

[41]Therefore the Jews started complaining about Him because He said, "I am the bread that came down from heaven." [42]They were saying, "Isn't this Jesus the son of Joseph, whose father and mother we know? How can He now say, 'I have come down from heaven'?"

[43]Jesus answered them, "Stop complaining among yourselves. [44]No one can come to Me unless the Father who sent Me draws[A] him, and I will raise him up on the last day. [45]It is written in the Prophets: **And they will all be taught by God.**[B] Everyone who has listened to and learned from the Father comes to Me— [46]not that anyone has seen the Father except the One who is from God. He has seen the Father.

[47]"I assure you: Anyone who believes[C] has eternal life. [48]I am the bread of life. [49]Your fathers ate the manna in the wilderness, and they died. [50]This is the bread that comes down from heaven so that anyone may eat of it and not die. [51]I am the living bread that came down from heaven. If anyone eats of this bread he will live forever. The bread that I will give for the life of the world is My flesh."

[52]At that, the Jews argued among themselves, "How can this man give us His flesh to eat?"

[53]So Jesus said to them, "I assure you: Unless you eat the flesh of the Son of Man and drink His blood, you do not have life in yourselves. [54]Anyone who eats My flesh and drinks My blood has eternal life, and I will raise him up on the last day, [55]because My flesh is real food and My blood is real drink. [56]The one who eats My flesh and drinks My blood lives in Me, and I in him. [57]Just as the living Father sent Me and I live because of the Father, so the one who feeds on Me will live because of Me. [58]This is the bread that came down from heaven; it is not like the manna[D] your fathers ate—and they died. The one who eats this bread will live forever."

[59]He said these things while teaching in the synagogue in Capernaum.

[60]Therefore, when many of His disciples heard this, they said, "This teaching is hard! Who can accept[E] it?"

[61]Jesus, knowing in Himself that His disciples were complaining about this, asked them, "Does this offend you? [62]Then what if you were to observe the Son of Man ascending to where He was before? [63]The Spirit is the One who gives life. The flesh doesn't help at all. The words that I have spoken to you are spirit and are life. [64]But there are some among you who don't believe." (For Jesus knew from the beginning those who would not[F] believe and the one who would betray Him.) [65]He said, "This is why I told you that no one can come to Me unless it is granted to him by the Father."

[66]From that moment many of His disciples turned back and no longer accompanied Him. [67]Therefore Jesus said to the Twelve, "You don't want to go away too, do you?"

[68]Simon Peter answered, "Lord, who will we go to? You have the words of eternal life. [69]We have come to believe and know that You are the Holy One of God!"[G]

[70]Jesus replied to them, "Didn't I choose you, the Twelve? Yet one of you is the Devil!" [71]He was referring to Judas, Simon Iscariot's son,[H,I] one of the Twelve, because he was going to betray Him.

7 After this, Jesus traveled in Galilee, since He did not want to travel in Judea because the Jews were trying to kill Him. [2]The Jewish Festival of Tabernacles[J,K] was near, [3]so His brothers said to Him, "Leave here and go to Judea so Your disciples can see Your works that You are doing. [4]For no one does anything in secret while he's seeking public recognition. If You do these things, show Yourself to the world." [5](For not even His brothers believed in Him.)

[6]Jesus told them, "My time has not yet arrived, but your time is always at hand. [7]The world cannot hate you, but it does hate Me because I testify about it—that its deeds are evil. [8]Go up to the festival yourselves. I'm not going up to the festival yet,[L] because My time has not yet fully come." [9]After He had said these things, He stayed in Galilee.

[10]After His brothers had gone up to the festival, then He also went up, not openly but

A6:44 Or *brings*, or *leads*; see the use of this Gk verb in Jn 12:32; 21:6; Ac 16:19; Jms 2:6. B6:45 Is 54:13 C6:47 Other mss add *in Me* D6:58 Other mss omit *the manna* E6:60 Lit *hear* F6:64 Other mss omit *not* G6:69 Other mss read *You are the Messiah, the Son of the Living God* H6:71 Other mss read *Judas Iscariot, Simon's son* I6:71 Lit *Judas, of Simon Iscariot* J7:2 Or *Booths* K7:2 One of 3 great Jewish religious festivals, along with Passover and Pentecost; Ex 23:14; Dt 16:16 L7:8 Other mss omit *yet* secretly. ¹¹The Jews were looking for Him at the festival and saying, "Where is He?" ¹²And there was a lot of discussion about Him among the crowds. Some were saying, "He's a good man." Others were saying, "No, on the contrary, He's deceiving the people." ¹³Still, nobody was talking publicly about Him because they feared the Jews.

¹⁴When the festival was already half over, Jesus went up into the temple complex and began to teach. ¹⁵Then the Jews were amazed and said, "How does He know the Scriptures, since He hasn't been trained?"

¹⁶Jesus answered them, "My teaching isn't Mine but is from the One who sent Me. ¹⁷If anyone wants to do His will, he will understand whether the teaching is from God or if I am speaking on My own. ¹⁸The one who speaks for himself seeks his own glory. But He who seeks the glory of the One who sent Him is true, and there is no unrighteousness in Him. ¹⁹Didn't Moses give you the law? Yet none of you keeps the law! Why do you want to kill Me?"

²⁰"You have a demon!" the crowd responded. "Who wants to kill You?"

²¹"I did one work, and you are all amazed," Jesus answered. ²²"Consider this: Moses has given you circumcision—not that it comes from Moses but from the fathers—and you circumcise a man on the Sabbath. ²³If a man receives circumcision on the Sabbath so that the law of Moses won't be broken, are you angry at Me because I made a man entirely well on the Sabbath? ²⁴Stop judging according to outward appearances; rather judge according to righteous judgment."

²⁵Some of the people of Jerusalem were saying, "Isn't this the man they want to kill? ²⁶Yet, look! He's speaking publicly and they're saying nothing to Him. Can it be true that the authorities know He is the Messiah? ²⁷But we know where this man is from. When the Messiah comes, nobody will know where He is from."

²⁸As He was teaching in the temple complex, Jesus cried out, "You know Me and you know where I am from. Yet I have not come on My own, but the One who sent Me is true. You don't know Him; ²⁹I know Him because I am from Him, and He sent Me."

³⁰Then they tried to seize Him. Yet no one laid a hand on Him because His hour^A had not yet come. ³¹However, many from the crowd believed in Him and said, "When the Messiah comes, He won't perform more signs than this man has done, will He?"

³²The Pharisees heard the crowd muttering these things about Him, so the chief priests and the Pharisees sent temple police to arrest Him.

³³Then Jesus said, "I am only with you for a short time. Then I'm going to the One who sent Me. ³⁴You will look for Me, but you will not find Me; and where I am, you cannot come."

³⁵Then the Jews said to one another, "Where does He intend to go so we won't find Him? He doesn't intend to go to the Dispersion^B among the Greeks and teach the Greeks, does He? ³⁶What is this remark He made: 'You will look for Me, and you will not find Me; and where I am, you cannot come'?"

³⁷On the last and most important day of the festival, Jesus stood up and cried out, "If anyone is thirsty, he should come to Me^C and drink! ³⁸The one who believes in Me, as the Scripture has said,^D will have streams of living water flow from deep within him." ³⁹He said this about the Spirit. Those who believed in Jesus were going to receive the Spirit, for the Spirit^E had not yet been received^F,G because Jesus had not yet been glorified.

⁴⁰When some from the crowd heard these words, they said, "This really is the Prophet!"^H ⁴¹Others said, "This is the Messiah!" But some said, "Surely the Messiah doesn't come from Galilee, does He? ⁴²Doesn't the Scripture say that the Messiah comes from David's offspring^I and from the town of Bethlehem, where David once lived?" ⁴³So a division occurred among the crowd because of Him. ⁴⁴Some of them wanted to seize Him, but no one laid hands on Him.

⁴⁵Then the temple police came to the chief priests and Pharisees, who asked them, "Why haven't you brought Him?"

⁴⁶The police answered, "No man ever spoke like this!"^J

⁴⁷Then the Pharisees responded to them: "Are you fooled too? ⁴⁸Have any of the rulers or

^A7:30 The time of His sacrificial death and exaltation; Jn 2:4; 8:20; 12:23,27; 13:1; 17:1   ^B7:35 Jewish people scattered throughout Gentile lands who spoke Gk and were influenced by Gk culture   ^C7:37 Other mss omit *to Me*   ^D7:38 Jesus may have had several OT passages in mind; Is 58:11; Ezk 47:1-12; Zch 14:8   ^E7:39 Other mss read *Holy Spirit*   ^F7:39 Other mss read *had not yet been given*   ^G7:39 Lit *the Spirit was not yet*; the word *received* is implied from the previous clause.   ^H7:40 Probably the Prophet in Dt 18:15   ^I7:42 Lit *seed*   ^J7:46 Other mss read *like this man*

Pharisees believed in Him? [49] But this crowd, which doesn't know the law, is accursed!"

[50] Nicodemus—the one who came to Him previously, being one of them—said to them, [51] "Our law doesn't judge a man before it hears from him and knows what he's doing, does it?"

[52] "You aren't from Galilee too, are you?" they replied. "Investigate and you will see that no prophet arises from Galilee."[A]

8 [[53] So each one went to his house. [1] But Jesus went to the Mount of Olives.

[2] At dawn He went to the temple complex again, and all the people were coming to Him. He sat down and began to teach them.

[3] Then the scribes and the Pharisees brought a woman caught in adultery, making her stand in the center. [4] "Teacher," they said to Him, "this woman was caught in the act of committing adultery. [5] In the law Moses commanded us to stone such women. So what do You say?" [6] They asked this to trap Him, in order that they might have evidence to accuse Him.

Jesus stooped down and started writing on the ground with His finger. [7] When they persisted in questioning Him, He stood up and said to them, "The one without sin among you should be the first to throw a stone at her."

[8] Then He stooped down again and continued writing on the ground. [9] When they heard this, they left one by one, starting with the older men. Only He was left, with the woman in the center. [10] When Jesus stood up, He said to her, "Woman, where are they? Has no one condemned you?"

[11] "No one, Lord,"[B] she answered.

"Neither do I condemn you," said Jesus. "Go, and from now on do not sin anymore."][C]

[12] Then Jesus spoke to them again: "I am the light of the world. Anyone who follows Me will never walk in the darkness but will have the light of life."

[13] So the Pharisees said to Him, "You are testifying about Yourself. Your testimony is not valid."[D]

[14] "Even if I testify about Myself," Jesus replied, "My testimony is valid,[E] because I know where I came from and where I'm going. But you don't know where I come from or where I'm going. [15] You judge by human standards.[F] I judge no one. [16] And if I do judge, My judg-

ment is true, because I am not alone, but I and the Father who sent Me judge together. [17] Even in your law it is written that the witness of two men is valid. [18] I am the One who testifies about Myself, and the Father who sent Me testifies about Me."

[19] Then they asked Him, "Where is Your Father?"

"You know neither Me nor My Father," Jesus answered. "If you knew Me, you would also know My Father." [20] He spoke these words by the treasury,[G] while teaching in the temple complex. But no one seized Him, because His hour[H] had not come.

[21] Then He said to them again, "I'm going away; you will look for Me, and you will die in your sin. Where I'm going, you cannot come."

[22] So the Jews said again, "He won't kill Himself, will He, since He says, 'Where I'm going, you cannot come'?"

[23] "You are from below," He told them, "I am from above. You are of this world; I am not of this world. [24] Therefore I told you that you will die in your sins. For if you do not believe that I am He,[I] you will die in your sins."

[25] "Who are You?" they questioned.

"Precisely what I've been telling you from the very beginning," Jesus told them. [26] "I have many things to say and to judge about you, but the One who sent Me is true, and what I have heard from Him—these things I tell the world."

[27] They did not know He was speaking to them about the Father. [28] So Jesus said to them, "When you lift up the Son of Man, then you will know that I am He, and that I do nothing on My own. But just as the Father taught Me, I say these things. [29] The One who sent Me is with Me. He has not left Me alone, because I always do what pleases Him."

[30] As He was saying these things, many believed in Him. [31] So Jesus said to the Jews who had believed Him, "If you continue in My word,[J] you really are My disciples. [32] You will know the truth, and the truth will set you free."

[33] "We are descendants[K] of Abraham," they answered Him, "and we have never been enslaved to anyone. How can You say, 'You will become free'?"

[A]7:52 Jonah and probably other prophets did come from Galilee; 2Kg 14:25 [B]8:11 Or *Sir*; Jn 4:15,49; 5:7, 6:34; 9:36 [C]8:11 Other mss omit bracketed text [D]8:13 The law of Moses required at least 2 witnesses to make a claim legally valid (v. 17). [E]8:14 Or *true* [F]8:15 Lit *You judge according to the flesh* [G]8:20 A place for offerings to be given, perhaps in the court of women [H]8:20 The time of His sacrificial death and exaltation; Jn 2:4; 7:30; 12:23,27; 13:1; 17:1 [I]8:24 Jesus claimed to be deity, but the Pharisees didn't understand His meaning. [J]8:31 Or *My teaching*, or *My message* [K]8:33, Or *offspring*; lit *seed*; Jn 7:42

³⁴Jesus responded, "I assure you: Everyone who commits sin is a slave of sin. ³⁵A slave does not remain in the household forever, but a son does remain forever. ³⁶Therefore, if the Son sets you free, you really will be free. ³⁷I know you are descendants^A of Abraham, but you are trying to kill Me because My word^B is not welcome among you. ³⁸I speak what I have seen in the presence of the Father;^C therefore, you do what you have heard from your father."

³⁹"Our father is Abraham!" they replied.

"If you were Abraham's children," Jesus told them, "you would do what Abraham did. ⁴⁰But now you are trying to kill Me, a man who has told you the truth that I heard from God. Abraham did not do this! ⁴¹You're doing what your father does."

"We weren't born of sexual immorality," they said. "We have one Father—God."

⁴²Jesus said to them, "If God were your Father, you would love Me, because I came from God and I am here. For I didn't come on My own, but He sent Me. ⁴³Why don't you understand what I say? Because you cannot listen to^D My word. ⁴⁴You are of your father the Devil, and you want to carry out your father's desires. He was a murderer from the beginning and has not stood in the truth, because there is no truth in him. When he tells a lie, he speaks from his own nature,^E because he is a liar and the father of liars.^F ⁴⁵Yet because I tell the truth, you do not believe Me. ⁴⁶Who among you can convict Me of sin? If I tell the truth, why don't you believe Me? ⁴⁷The one who is from God listens to God's words. This is why you don't listen, because you are not from God."

⁴⁸The Jews responded to Him, "Aren't we right in saying that You're a Samaritan and have a demon?"

⁴⁹"I do not have a demon," Jesus answered. "On the contrary, I honor My Father and you dishonor Me. ⁵⁰I do not seek My glory; the One who seeks it also judges. ⁵¹I assure you: If anyone keeps My word, he will never see death—ever!"

⁵²Then the Jews said, "Now we know You have a demon. Abraham died and so did the prophets. You say, 'If anyone keeps My word, he will never taste death—ever!' ⁵³Are You

greater than our father Abraham who died? Even the prophets died. Who do You pretend to be?"^G

⁵⁴"If I glorify Myself," Jesus answered, "My glory is nothing. My Father—you say about Him, 'He is our God'—He is the One who glorifies Me. ⁵⁵You've never known Him, but I know Him. If I were to say I don't know Him, I would be a liar like you. But I do know Him, and I keep His word. ⁵⁶Your father Abraham was overjoyed that he would see My day; he saw it and rejoiced."

⁵⁷The Jews replied, "You aren't 50 years old yet, and You've seen Abraham?"^H

⁵⁸Jesus said to them, "I assure you: Before Abraham was, I am."^I

⁵⁹At that, they picked up stones to throw at Him. But Jesus was hidden^J and went out of the temple complex.^K

9 As He was passing by, He saw a man blind from birth. ²His disciples questioned Him: "Rabbi, who sinned, this man or his parents, that he was born blind?"

³"Neither this man nor his parents sinned," Jesus answered. "This came about so that God's works might be displayed in him. ⁴We^L must do the works of Him who sent Me^M while it is day. Night is coming when no one can work. ⁵As long as I am in the world, I am the light of the world."

⁶After He said these things He spit on the ground, made some mud from the saliva, and spread the mud on his eyes. ⁷"Go," He told him, "wash in the pool of Siloam" (which means "Sent"). So he left, washed, and came back seeing.

⁸His neighbors and those who formerly had seen him as a beggar said, "Isn't this the man who sat begging?" ⁹Some said, "He's the one." "No," others were saying, "but he looks like him."

He kept saying, "I'm the one!"

¹⁰Therefore they asked him, "Then how were your eyes opened?"

¹¹He answered, "The man called Jesus made mud, spread it on my eyes, and told me, 'Go to Siloam and wash.' So when I went and washed I received my sight."

¹²"Where is He?" they asked.

"I don't know," he said.

^A8:37 Or My teaching, or My message   ^B8:37, Or offspring; lit seed; Jn 7:42   ^C8:38 Other mss read of   My Father   ^D8:43 Or cannot hear   ^E8:44 Lit from his own things   ^F8:44 Lit of it   ^G8:53 Lit Who do You make Yourself?   ^H8:57 Other mss read and Abraham has seen You?   ^I8:58 I AM is the name God gave Himself at the burning bush; Ex 3:13-14; see note at Jn 8:24.   ^J8:59 Or Jesus hid Himself   ^K8:59 Other mss add and having gone through their midst, He passed by   ^L9:4 Other mss read I   ^M9:4 Other mss read sent us

[13] They brought the man who used to be blind to the Pharisees. [14] The day that Jesus made the mud and opened his eyes was a Sabbath. [15] So again the Pharisees asked him how he received his sight.

"He put mud on my eyes," he told them. "I washed and I can see."

[16] Therefore some of the Pharisees said, "This man is not from God, for He doesn't keep the Sabbath!" But others were saying, "How can a sinful man perform such signs?" And there was a division among them.

[17] Again they asked the blind man,[A] "What do you say about Him, since He opened your eyes?"

"He's a prophet," he said.

[18] The Jews did not believe this about him —that he was blind and received sight—until they summoned the parents of the one who had received his sight. [19] They asked them, "Is this your son, the one you say was born blind? How then does he now see?"

[20] "We know this is our son and that he was born blind," his parents answered. [21] "But we don't know how he now sees, and we don't know who opened his eyes. Ask him; he's of age. He will speak for himself." [22] His parents said these things because they were afraid of the Jews, since the Jews had already agreed that if anyone confessed Him as Messiah, he would be banned from the synagogue. [23] This is why his parents said, "He's of age; ask him."

[24] So a second time they summoned the man who had been blind and told him, "Give glory to God.[B] We know that this man is a sinner!"

[25] He answered, "Whether or not He's a sinner, I don't know. One thing I do know: I was blind, and now I can see!"

[26] Then they asked him, "What did He do to you? How did He open your eyes?"

[27] "I already told you," he said, "and you didn't listen. Why do you want to hear it again? You don't want to become His disciples too, do you?"

[28] They ridiculed him: "You're that man's disciple, but we're Moses' disciples. [29] We know that God has spoken to Moses. But this man—we don't know where He's from!"

[30] "This is an amazing thing," the man told them. "You don't know where He is from, yet He opened my eyes! [31] We know that God doesn't listen to sinners, but if anyone is God-fearing and does His will, He listens to him. [32] Throughout history[C] no one has ever heard of someone opening the eyes of a person born blind. [33] If this man were not from God, He wouldn't be able to do anything."

[34] "You were born entirely in sin," they replied, "and are you trying to teach us?" Then they threw him out.[D]

[35] When Jesus heard that they had thrown the man out, He found him and asked, "Do you believe in the Son of Man?"[E]

[36] "Who is He, Sir, that I may believe in Him?" he asked.

[37] Jesus answered, "You have seen Him; in fact, He is the One speaking with you."

[38] "I believe, Lord!" he said, and he worshiped Him.

[39] Jesus said, "I came into this world for judgment, in order that those who do not see will see and those who do see will become blind."

[40] Some of the Pharisees who were with Him heard these things and asked Him, "We aren't blind too, are we?"

[41] "If you were blind," Jesus told them, "you wouldn't have sin.[F] But now that you say, 'We see'—your sin remains.

10 "I assure you: Anyone who doesn't enter the sheep pen by the door but climbs in some other way, is a thief and a robber. [2] The one who enters by the door is the shepherd of the sheep. [3] The doorkeeper opens it for him, and the sheep hear his voice. He calls his own sheep by name and leads them out. [4] When he has brought all his own outside, he goes ahead of them. The sheep follow him because they recognize his voice. [5] They will never follow a stranger; instead they will run away from him, because they don't recognize the voice of strangers."

[6] Jesus gave them this illustration, but they did not understand what He was telling them.

[7] So Jesus said again, "I assure you: I am the door of the sheep. [8] All who came before Me[G] are thieves and robbers, but the sheep didn't listen to them. [9] I am the door. If anyone enters by Me, he will be saved and will come in and go out and find pasture. [10] A thief comes only to steal and to kill and to destroy. I have come so that they may have life and have it in abundance.

[A] 9:17 = the man who had been blind   [B] 9:24 *Give glory to God* was a solemn charge to tell the truth; Jos 7:19.   [C] 9:32 Lit *From the age*
[D] 9:34 = they banned him from the synagogue; v. 22   [E] 9:35 Other mss read *the Son of God*   [F] 9:41 To *have sin* is an idiom that refers to guilt
caused by sin.   [G] 10:8 Other mss omit *before Me*

¹¹"I am the good shepherd. The good shepherd lays down his life for the sheep. ¹²The hired man, since he is not the shepherd and doesn't own the sheep, leaves them^A and runs away when he sees a wolf coming. The wolf then snatches and scatters them. ¹³This happens because he is a hired man and doesn't care about the sheep.

¹⁴"I am the good shepherd. I know My own sheep, and they know Me, ¹⁵as the Father knows Me, and I know the Father. I lay down My life for the sheep. ¹⁶But I have other sheep that are not of this fold; I must bring them also, and they will listen to My voice. Then there will be one flock, one shepherd. ¹⁷This is why the Father loves Me, because I am laying down My life so I may take it up again. ¹⁸No one takes it from Me, but I lay it down on My own. I have the right to lay it down, and I have the right to take it up again. I have received this command from My Father."

¹⁹Again a division took place among the Jews because of these words. ²⁰Many of them were saying, "He has a demon and He's crazy! Why do you listen to Him?" ²¹Others were saying, "These aren't the words of someone demon-possessed. Can a demon open the eyes of the blind?"

²²Then the Festival of Dedication^B took place in Jerusalem, and it was winter. ²³Jesus was walking in the temple complex in Solomon's Colonnade.^C ²⁴Then the Jews surrounded Him and asked, "How long are You going to keep us in suspense?^D If You are the Messiah, tell us plainly."^E

²⁵"I did tell you and you don't believe," Jesus answered them. "The works that I do in My Father's name testify about Me. ²⁶But you don't believe because you are not My sheep.^F ²⁷My sheep hear My voice, I know them, and they follow Me. ²⁸I give them eternal life, and they will never perish—ever! No one will snatch them out of My hand. ²⁹My Father, who has given them to Me, is greater than all. No one is able to snatch them out of the Father's hand. ³⁰The Father and I are one."^G

³¹Again the Jews picked up rocks to stone Him.

³²Jesus replied, "I have shown you many good works from the Father. Which of these works are you stoning Me for?"

³³"We aren't stoning You for a good work," the Jews answered, "but for blasphemy, because You—being a man—make Yourself God."

³⁴Jesus answered them, "Isn't it written in your scripture,^H I said, you are gods?^I ³⁵If He called those whom the word of God came to 'gods'—and the Scripture cannot be broken— ³⁶do you say, 'You are blaspheming' to the One the Father set apart and sent into the world, because I said: I am the Son of God? ³⁷If I am not doing My Father's works, don't believe Me. ³⁸But if I am doing them and you don't believe Me, believe the works. This way you will know and understand^J that the Father is in Me and I in the Father." ³⁹Then they were trying again to seize Him, yet He eluded their grasp.

⁴⁰So He departed again across the Jordan to the place where John had been baptizing earlier, and He remained there. ⁴¹Many came to Him and said, "John never did a sign, but everything John said about this man was true." ⁴²And many believed in Him there.

11 Now a man was sick, Lazarus, from Bethany, the village of Mary and her sister Martha. ²Mary was the one who anointed the Lord with fragrant oil and wiped His feet with her hair, and it was her brother Lazarus who was sick. ³So the sisters sent a message to Him: "Lord, the one You love is sick."

⁴When Jesus heard it, He said, "This sickness will not end in death but is for the glory of God, so that the Son of God may be glorified through it." ⁵Now Jesus loved Martha, her sister, and Lazarus. ⁶So when He heard that he was sick, He stayed two more days in the place where He was. ⁷Then after that, He said to the disciples, "Let's go to Judea again."

⁸"Rabbi," the disciples told Him, "just now the Jews tried to stone You, and You're going there again?"

⁹"Aren't there 12 hours in a day?" Jesus answered. "If anyone walks during the day, he doesn't stumble, because he sees the light of this world. ¹⁰If anyone walks during the night, he does stumble, because the light is not in him." ¹¹He said this, and then He told them, "Our friend Lazarus has fallen asleep, but I'm on My way to wake him up."

^A**10:12** Lit *leaves the sheep*   ^B**10:22** Or *Hanukkah*, also called the *Feast of Lights*; this festival commemorated the rededication of the temple in 164 B.C.   ^C**10:23** Rows of columns supporting a roof   ^D**10:24** Lit *How long are you taking away our life?*   ^E**10:24** Or *openly*, or *publicly*   ^F**10:26** Other mss add *just as I told you*   ^G**10:30** Lit *I and the Father—We are one.*   ^H**10:34** Other mss read *in the scripture*   ^I**10:34** Ps 82:6   ^J**10:38** Other mss read *know and believe*

¹²Then the disciples said to Him, "Lord, if he has fallen asleep, he will get well."

¹³Jesus, however, was speaking about his death, but they thought He was speaking about natural sleep. ¹⁴So Jesus then told them plainly, "Lazarus has died. ¹⁵I'm glad for you that I wasn't there so that you may believe. But let's go to him."

¹⁶Then Thomas (called "Twin") said to his fellow disciples, "Let's go so that we may die with Him."

¹⁷When Jesus arrived, He found that Lazarus had already been in the tomb four days. ¹⁸Bethany was near Jerusalem (about two miles[A] away). ¹⁹Many of the Jews had come to Martha and Mary to comfort them about their brother. ²⁰As soon as Martha heard that Jesus was coming, she went to meet Him. But Mary remained seated in the house.

²¹Then Martha said to Jesus, "Lord, if You had been here, my brother wouldn't have died. ²²Yet even now I know that whatever You ask from God, God will give You."

²³"Your brother will rise again," Jesus told her.

²⁴Martha said, "I know that he will rise again in the resurrection at the last day."

²⁵Jesus said to her, "I am the resurrection and the life. The one who believes in Me, even if he dies, will live. ²⁶Everyone who lives and believes in Me will never die—ever. Do you believe this?"

²⁷"Yes, Lord," she told Him, "I believe You are the Messiah, the Son of God, who comes into the world."

²⁸Having asked this, she went back and called her sister Mary, saying in private, "The Teacher is here and is calling for you."

²⁹As soon as she heard this, she got up quickly and went to Him. ³⁰Jesus had not yet come into the village but was still in the place where Martha had met Him. ³¹The Jews who were with her in the house consoling her saw that Mary got up quickly and went out. So they followed her, supposing that she was going to the tomb to cry there.

³²When Mary came to where Jesus was and saw Him, she fell at His feet and told Him, "Lord, if You had been here, my brother would not have died!"

³³When Jesus saw her crying, and the Jews who had come with her crying, He was angry[B] in His spirit and deeply moved. ³⁴"Where have you put him?" He asked.

"Lord," they told Him, "come and see."

³⁵Jesus wept.

³⁶So the Jews said, "See how He loved him!" ³⁷But some of them said, "Couldn't He who opened the blind man's eyes also have kept this man from dying?"

³⁸Then Jesus, angry[C] in Himself again, came to the tomb. It was a cave, and a stone was lying against it. ³⁹"Remove the stone," Jesus said.

Martha, the dead man's sister, told Him, "Lord, he's already decaying.[D] It's been four days."

⁴⁰Jesus said to her, "Didn't I tell you that if you believed you would see the glory of God?"

⁴¹So they removed the stone. Then Jesus raised His eyes and said, "Father, I thank You that You heard Me. ⁴²I know that You always hear Me, but because of the crowd standing here I said this, so they may believe You sent Me." ⁴³After He said this, He shouted with a loud voice, "Lazarus, come out!" ⁴⁴The dead man came out bound hand and foot with linen strips and with his face wrapped in a cloth. Jesus said to them, "Loose him and let him go."

⁴⁵Therefore, many of the Jews who came to Mary and saw what He did believed in Him. ⁴⁶But some of them went to the Pharisees and told them what Jesus had done.

⁴⁷So the chief priests and the Pharisees convened the Sanhedrin and said, "What are we going to do since this man does many signs? ⁴⁸If we let Him continue in this way, everyone will believe in Him! Then the Romans will come and remove both our place[E] and our nation."

⁴⁹One of them, Caiaphas, who was high priest that year, said to them, "You know nothing at all! ⁵⁰You're not considering that it is to your[F] advantage that one man should die for the people rather than the whole nation perish." ⁵¹He did not say this on his own, but being high priest that year he prophesied that Jesus was going to die for the nation, ⁵²and not for the nation only, but also to unite the scattered children of God. ⁵³So from that day on

---

[A]11:18 Lit 15 stadia; 1 stadion = 600 feet   [B]11:33 The Gk word is very strong and probably indicates Jesus' anger against sin's tyranny and death.   [C]11:38 See note at 11:33.   [D]11:39 Lit he already stinks   [E]11:48 The temple or possibly all of Jerusalem   [F]11:50 Other mss read to our

they plotted to kill Him. ⁵⁴Therefore Jesus no longer walked openly among the Jews but departed from there to the countryside near the wilderness, to a town called Ephraim. And He stayed there with the disciples.

⁵⁵The Jewish Passover was near, and many went up to Jerusalem from the country to purify^A themselves before the Passover. ⁵⁶They were looking for Jesus and asking one another as they stood in the temple complex: "What do you think? He won't come to the festival, will He?" ⁵⁷The chief priests and the Pharisees had given orders that if anyone knew where He was, he should report it so they could arrest Him.

12 Six days before the Passover, Jesus came to Bethany where Lazarus^B was, the one Jesus had raised from the dead. ²So they gave a dinner for Him there; Martha was serving them, and Lazarus was one of those reclining at the table with Him. ³Then Mary took a pound of fragrant oil—pure and expensive nard—anointed Jesus' feet, and wiped His feet with her hair. So the house was filled with the fragrance of the oil.

⁴Then one of His disciples, Judas Iscariot (who was about to betray Him), said, ⁵"Why wasn't this fragrant oil sold for 300 denarii^C and given to the poor?" ⁶He didn't say this because he cared about the poor but because he was a thief. He was in charge of the money-bag and would steal part of what was put in it.

⁷Jesus answered, "Leave her alone; she has kept it for the day of My burial. ⁸For you always have the poor with you, but you do not always have Me."

⁹Then a large crowd of the Jews learned He was there. They came not only because of Jesus, but also to see Lazarus the one He had raised from the dead. ¹⁰Therefore the chief priests decided to kill Lazarus also ¹¹because he was the reason many of the Jews were deserting them^D and believing in Jesus.

¹²The next day, when the large crowd that had come to the festival heard that Jesus was coming to Jerusalem, ¹³they took palm branches and went out to meet Him. They kept shouting: "*Hosanna!* **He who comes in the name of the Lord is the blessed One**^E—the King of Israel!"

¹⁴Jesus found a young donkey and sat on it, just as it is written: ¹⁵**Fear no more, Daughter Zion. Look, your King is coming, sitting on a donkey's colt.**^F

¹⁶His disciples did not understand these things at first. However, when Jesus was glorified, then they remembered that these things had been written about Him and that they had done these things to Him. ¹⁷Meanwhile, the crowd, which had been with Him when He called Lazarus out of the tomb and raised him from the dead, continued to testify.^G ¹⁸This is also why the crowd met Him, because they heard He had done this sign.

¹⁹Then the Pharisees said to one another, "You see? You've accomplished nothing. Look—the world has gone after Him!"

²⁰Now some Greeks were among those who went up to worship at the festival. ²¹So they came to Philip, who was from Bethsaida in Galilee, and requested of him, "Sir, we want to see Jesus."

²²Philip went and told Andrew; then Andrew and Philip went and told Jesus. ²³Jesus replied to them, "The hour has come for the Son of Man to be glorified.

²⁴"I assure you: Unless a grain of wheat falls to the ground and dies, it remains by itself. But if it dies, it produces a large crop.^H ²⁵The one who loves his life will lose it, and the one who hates his life in this world will keep it for eternal life. ²⁶If anyone serves Me, he must follow Me. Where I am, there My servant also will be. If anyone serves Me, the Father will honor him.

²⁷"Now My soul is troubled. What should I say—Father, save Me from this hour? But that is why I came to this hour. ²⁸Father, glorify Your name!"^I

Then a voice came from heaven: "I have glorified it, and I will glorify it again!"

²⁹The crowd standing there heard it and said it was thunder. Others said that an angel had spoken to Him.

³⁰Jesus responded, "This voice came, not for Me, but for you. ³¹Now is the judgment of this world. Now the ruler of this world will be cast out. ³²As for Me, if I am lifted up^J from the earth I will draw all people to Myself." ³³He

^A**11:55** The law of Moses required God's people to purify or cleanse themselves so they could celebrate the Passover. Jews often came to Jerusalem a week early to do this; Nm 9:4-11.   ^B**12:1** Other mss read *Lazarus who died*   ^C**12:5** This amount was about a year's wages for a common worker.   ^D**12:11** Lit *going away*   ^E**12:13** Ps 118:25-26   ^F**12:15** Zch 9:9   ^G**12:17** Other mss read *Meanwhile the crowd, which had been with Him, continued to testify that He had called Lazarus out of the tomb and raised him from the dead.*   ^H**12:24** Lit *produces much fruit*   ^I**12:28** Other mss read *Your Son*   ^J**12:32** Or *exalted*

said this to signify what kind of death He was about to die.

³⁴Then the crowd replied to Him, "We have heard from the scripture that the Messiah will remain forever. So how can You say, 'The Son of Man must be lifted up'?ᴬ Who is this Son of Man?"

³⁵Jesus answered, "The light will be with you only a little longer. Walk while you have the light so that darkness doesn't overtake you. The one who walks in darkness doesn't know where he's going. ³⁶While you have the light, believe in the light so that you may become sons of light." Jesus said this, then went away and hid from them.

³⁷Even though He had performed so many signs in their presence, they did not believe in Him. ³⁸But this was to fulfill the word of Isaiah the prophet, who said:ᴮ

> **Lord, who has believed**
> **our message?**
> **And who has the arm of the Lord**
> **been revealed to?**ᶜ

³⁹This is why they were unable to believe, because Isaiah also said:

> ⁴⁰ **He has blinded their eyes**
> **and hardened their hearts,**
> **so that they would not see**
> **with their eyes**
> **or understand with their hearts,**
> **and be converted,**
> **and I would heal them.**ᴰ

⁴¹Isaiah said these things becauseᴱ he saw His glory and spoke about Him.

⁴²Nevertheless, many did believe in Him even among the rulers, but because of the Pharisees they did not confess Him, so they would not be banned from the synagogue. ⁴³For they loved praise from men more than praise from God.ᶠ

⁴⁴Then Jesus cried out, "The one who believes in Me believes not in Me, but in Him who sent Me. ⁴⁵And the one who sees Me sees Him who sent Me. ⁴⁶I have come as a light into the world, so that everyone who believes in Me would not remain in darkness. ⁴⁷If anyone hears My words and doesn't keep them, I do not judge him; for I did not come to judge the world but to save the world. ⁴⁸The one who

rejects Me and doesn't accept My sayings has this as his judge:ᴳ The word I have spoken will judge him on the last day. ⁴⁹For I have not spoken on My own, but the Father Himself who sent Me has given Me a command as to what I should say and what I should speak. ⁵⁰I know that His command is eternal life. So the things that I speak, I speak just as the Father has told Me."

13 Before the Passover Festival, Jesus knew that His hour had come to depart from this world to the Father. Having loved His own who were in the world, He loved them to the end.ᴴ

²Now by the time of supper, the Devil had already put it into the heart of Judas, Simon Iscariot's son, to betray Him. ³Jesus knew that the Father had given everything into His hands, that He had come from God, and that He was going back to God. ⁴So He got up from supper, laid aside His robe, took a towel, and tied it around Himself. ⁵Next, He poured water into a basin and began to wash His disciples' feet and to dry them with the towel tied around Him.

⁶He came to Simon Peter, who asked Him, "Lord, are You going to wash my feet?"

⁷Jesus answered him, "What I'm doing you don't understand now, but afterward you will know."

⁸"You will never wash my feet—ever!" Peter said.

Jesus replied, "If I don't wash you, you have no part with Me."

⁹Simon Peter said to Him, "Lord, not only my feet, but also my hands and my head."

¹⁰"One who has bathed," Jesus told him, "doesn't need to wash anything except his feet, but he is completely clean. You are clean, but not all of you." ¹¹For He knew who would betray Him. This is why He said, "You are not all clean."

¹²When Jesus had washed their feet and put on His robe, He reclinedᴵ again and said to them, "Do you know what I have done for you? ¹³You call Me Teacher and Lord. This is well said, for I am. ¹⁴So if I, your Lord and Teacher, have washed your feet, you also ought to wash one another's feet. ¹⁵For I have given you an example that you also should do just as I have done for you.

ᴬ**12:34** Or *exalted*   ᴮ**12:38** Lit *which he said*   ᶜ**12:38** Is 53:1   ᴰ**12:40** Is 6:10   ᴱ**12:41** Other mss read *when*   ᶠ**12:43** Lit *loved glory of men more than glory of God*; v. 41; Jn 5:41   ᴳ**12:48** Lit *has the one judging him*   ᴴ**13:1** = completely or always   ᴵ**13:12** At important meals the custom was to recline on a mat at a low table and lean on the left elbow.

¹⁶"I assure you: A slave is not greater than his master,ᴬ and a messenger is not greater than the one who sent him. ¹⁷If you know these things, you are blessed if you do them. ¹⁸I'm not speaking about all of you; I know those I have chosen. But the Scripture must be fulfilled: The one who eats My breadᴮ has raised his heel against Me.ᶜ

¹⁹"I am telling you now before it happens, so that when it does happen you will believe that I am He. ²⁰I assure you: Whoever receives anyone I send receives Me, and the one who receives Me receives Him who sent Me."

²¹When Jesus had said this, He was troubled in His spirit and testified, "I assure you: One of you will betray Me!"

²²The disciples started looking at one another—uncertain which one He was speaking about. ²³One of His disciples, the one Jesus loved, was reclining close beside Jesus.ᴰ ²⁴Simon Peter motioned to him to find out who it was He was talking about. ²⁵So he leaned back against Jesus and asked Him, "Lord, who is it?"

²⁶Jesus replied, "He's the one I give the piece of bread to after I have dipped it." When He had dipped the bread, He gave it to Judas, Simon Iscariot's son.ᴱ ²⁷After Judas ate the piece of bread, Satan entered him. Therefore Jesus told him, "What you're doing, do quickly."

²⁸None of those reclining at the table knew why He told him this. ²⁹Since Judas kept the money-bag, some thought that Jesus was telling him, "Buy what we need for the festival," or that he should give something to the poor. ³⁰After receiving the piece of bread, he went out immediately. And it was night.

³¹When he had gone out, Jesus said, "Now the Son of Man is glorified, and God is glorified in Him. ³²If God is glorified in Him,ᶠ God will also glorify Him in Himself and will glorify Him at once.

³³"Children, I am with you a little while longer. You will look for Me, and just as I told the Jews, 'Where I am going you cannot come,' so now I tell you.

³⁴"I give you a new command: Love one another. Just as I have loved you, you must also love one another. ³⁵By this all people will know

that you are My disciples, if you have love for one another."

³⁶"Lord," Simon Peter said to Him, "where are You going?"

Jesus answered, "Where I am going you cannot follow Me now, but you will follow later."

³⁷"Lord," Peter asked, "why can't I follow You now? I will lay down my life for You!"

³⁸Jesus replied, "Will you lay down your life for Me? I assure you: A rooster will not crow until you have denied Me three times.

14 "Your heart must not be troubled. Believeᴳ in God; believe also in Me. ²In My Father's house are many dwelling places;ᴴ if not, I would have told you. I am going away to prepare a place for you. ³If I go away and prepare a place for you, I will come back and receive you to Myself, so that where I am you may be also. ⁴You know the way to where I am going."ᴵ

⁵"Lord," Thomas said, "we don't know where You're going. How can we know the way?"

⁶Jesus told him, "I am the way, the truth, and the life. No one comes to the Father except through Me.

⁷"If you know Me, you will also knowᴶ My Father. From now on you do know Him and have seen Him."

⁸"Lord," said Philip, "show us the Father, and that's enough for us."

⁹Jesus said to him, "Have I been among you all this time without your knowing Me, Philip? The one who has seen Me has seen the Father. How can you say, 'Show us the Father'? ¹⁰Don't you believe that I am in the Father and the Father is in Me? The words I speak to you I do not speak on My own. The Father who lives in Me does His works. ¹¹Believe Me that I am in the Father and the Father is in Me. Otherwise, believeᴷ because of the works themselves.

¹²"I assure you: The one who believes in Me will also do the works that I do. And he will do even greater works than these, because I am going to the Father. ¹³Whatever you ask in My name, I will do it so that the Father may be glorified in the Son. ¹⁴If you ask Meᴸ anything in My name, I will do it.ᴹ

¹⁵"If you love Me, you will keepᴺ My commands. ¹⁶And I will ask the Father, and He will

ᴬ13:16 Or *lord*   ᴮ13:18 Other mss read *eats bread with Me*   ᶜ13:18 Ps 41:9   ᴰ13:23 Lit *reclining at Jesus' breast*; that is, on His right; Jn 1:18   ᴱ13:26 Other mss read *Judas Iscariot, Simon's son*   ᶠ13:32 Other mss omit *If God is glorified in Him*   ᴳ14:1 Or *You believe*   ᴴ14:2 The Vg used the Lat term *mansio*, a traveler's resting place. The Gk word is related to the verb *meno*, meaning *remain* or *stay*, which occurs 40 times in John.   ᴵ14:4 Other mss read this verse: *And you know where I am going, and you know the way*   ᴶ14:7 Other mss read *If you had known Me, you would have known*   ᴷ14:11 Other mss read *believe Me*   ᴸ14:14 Other mss omit *Me*   ᴹ14:14 Other mss omit all of v. 14   ᴺ14:15 Other mss read *If you love Me, keep* (as a command)

give you another Counselor to be with you forever. [17] He is the Spirit of truth. The world is unable to receive Him because it doesn't see Him or know Him. But you do know Him, because He remains with you and will be[A] in you. [18] I will not leave you as orphans; I am coming to you.

[19] "In a little while the world will see Me no longer, but you will see Me. Because I live, you will live too. [20] In that day you will know that I am in My Father, you are in Me, and I am in you. [21] The one who has My commands and keeps them is the one who loves Me. And the one who loves Me will be loved by My Father. I also will love him and will reveal Myself to him."

[22] Judas (not Iscariot) said to Him, "Lord, how is it You're going to reveal Yourself to us and not to the world?"

[23] Jesus answered, "If anyone loves Me, he will keep My word. My Father will love him, and We will come to him and make Our home with him. [24] The one who doesn't love Me will not keep My words. The word that you hear is not Mine but is from the Father who sent Me.

[25] "I have spoken these things to you while I remain with you. [26] But the Counselor, the Holy Spirit—the Father will send Him in My name—will teach you all things and remind you of everything I have told you.

[27] "Peace I leave with you. My peace I give to you. I do not give to you as the world gives. Your heart must not be troubled or fearful. [28] You have heard Me tell you, 'I am going away and I am coming to you.' If you loved Me, you would have rejoiced that I am going to the Father, because the Father is greater than I. [29] I have told you now before it happens so that when it does happen you may believe. [30] I will not talk with you much longer, because the ruler of the world is coming. He has no power over Me.[B] [31] On the contrary, I am going away[C] so that the world may know that I love the Father. Just as the Father commanded Me, so I do.

"Get up; let's leave this place.

15 "I am the true vine, and My Father is the vineyard keeper. [2] Every branch in Me that does not produce fruit He removes, and He prunes every branch that produces fruit so that it will produce more fruit. [3] You are already clean because of the word I have spoken

to you. [4] Remain in Me, and I in you. Just as a branch is unable to produce fruit by itself unless it remains on the vine, so neither can you unless you remain in Me.

[5] "I am the vine; you are the branches. The one who remains in Me and I in him produces much fruit, because you can do nothing without Me. [6] If anyone does not remain in Me, he is thrown aside like a branch and he withers. They gather them, throw them into the fire, and they are burned. [7] If you remain in Me and My words remain in you, ask whatever you want and it will be done for you. [8] My Father is glorified by this: that you produce much fruit and prove to be[D] My disciples.

[9] "As the Father has loved Me, I have also loved you. Remain in My love. [10] If you keep My commands you will remain in My love, just as I have kept My Father's commands and remain in His love.

[11] "I have spoken these things to you so that My joy may be in you and your joy may be complete. [12] This is My command: Love one another as I have loved you. [13] No one has greater love than this, that someone would lay down his life for his friends. [14] You are My friends if you do what I command you. [15] I do not call you slaves anymore, because a slave doesn't know what his master[E] is doing. I have called you friends, because I have made known to you everything I have heard from My Father. [16] You did not choose Me, but I chose you. I appointed you that you should go out and produce fruit and that your fruit should remain, so that whatever you ask the Father in My name, He will give you. [17] This is what I command you: Love one another.

[18] "If the world hates you, understand that it hated Me before it hated you. [19] If you were of the world, the world would love you as its own. However, because you are not of the world, but I have chosen you out of it, the world hates you. [20] Remember the word I spoke to you: 'A slave is not greater than his master.' If they persecuted Me, they will also persecute you. If they kept My word, they will also keep yours. [21] But they will do all these things to you on account of My name, because they don't know the One who sent Me. [22] If I had not come and spoken to them, they would not have sin.[F] Now they have no excuse for their sin. [23] The one who hates Me also hates My Father. [24] If I had not done the

works among them that no one else has done, they would not have sin. Now they have seen and hated both Me and My Father. ²⁵But this happened so that the statement written in their scripture might be fulfilled: They hated Me for no reason.ᴬ

²⁶"When the Counselor comes, the One I will send to you from the Father—the Spirit of truth who proceeds from the Father—He will testify about Me. ²⁷You also will testify, because you have been with Me from the beginning.

16 "I have told you these things to keep you from stumbling. ²They will ban you from the synagogues. In fact, a time is coming when anyone who kills you will think he is offering service to God. ³They will do these things because they haven't known the Father or Me. ⁴But I have told you these things so that when their timeᴮ comes you may remember I told them to you. I didn't tell you these things from the beginning, because I was with you.

⁵"But now I am going away to Him who sent Me, and not one of you asks Me, 'Where are You going?' ⁶Yet, because I have spoken these things to you, sorrow has filled your heart. ⁷Nevertheless, I am telling you the truth. It is for your benefit that I go away, because if I don't go away the Counselor will not come to you. If I go, I will send Him to you. ⁸When He comes, He will convict the world about sin, righteousness, and judgment: ⁹About sin, because they do not believe in Me; ¹⁰about righteousness, because I am going to the Father and you will no longer see Me; ¹¹and about judgment, because the ruler of this world has been judged.

¹²"I still have many things to tell you, but you can't bear them now. ¹³When the Spirit of truth comes, He will guide you into all the truth. For He will not speak on His own, but He will speak whatever He hears. He will also declare to you what is to come. ¹⁴He will glorify Me, because He will take from what is Mine and declare it to you. ¹⁵Everything the Father has is Mine. This is why I told you that He takes from what is Mine and will declare it to you.

¹⁶"A little while and you will no longer see Me; again a little while and you will see Me."ᶜ

¹⁷Therefore some of His disciples said to one another, "What is this He tells us: 'A little while and you will not see Me; again a little while and

you will see Me'; and, 'because I am going to the Father'?" ¹⁸They said, "What is this He is saying,ᴰ 'A little while'? We don't know what He's talking about!"

¹⁹Jesus knew they wanted to question Him, so He said to them, "Are you asking one another about what I said, 'A little while and you will not see Me; again a little while and you will see Me'? ²⁰"I assure you: You will weep and wail, but the world will rejoice. You will become sorrowful, but your sorrow will turn to joy. ²¹When a woman is in labor she has pain because her time has come. But when she has given birth to a child, she no longer remembers the suffering because of the joy that a person has been born into the world. ²²So you also have sorrowᴱ now. But I will see you again. Your hearts will rejoice, and no one will rob you of your joy. ²³In that day you will not ask Me anything.

"I assure you: Anything you ask the Father in My name, He will give you. ²⁴Until now you have asked for nothing in My name. Ask and you will receive, so that your joy may be complete.

²⁵"I have spoken these things to you in figures of speech. A time is coming when I will no longer speak to you in figures, but I will tell you plainly about the Father. ²⁶In that day you will ask in My name. I am not telling you that I will make requests to the Father on your behalf. ²⁷For the Father Himself loves you, because you have loved Me and have believed that I came from God.ᶠ ²⁸I came from the Father and have come into the world. Again, I am leaving the world and going to the Father."

²⁹"Ah!" His disciples said. "Now You're speaking plainly and not using any figurative language. ³⁰Now we know that You know everything and don't need anyone to question You. By this we believe that You came from God."

³¹Jesus responded to them, "Do you now believe? ³²Look: An hour is coming, and has come, when each of you will be scattered to his own home, and you will leave Me alone. Yet I am not alone, because the Father is with Me. ³³I have told you these things so that in Me you may have peace. You will have suffering in this world. Be courageous! I have conquered the world."

ᴬ15:25 Ps 69:4 ᴮ16:4 Other mss read *when the time* ᶜ16:16 Other mss add *because I am going to the Father* ᴰ16:18 Other mss omit *He is saying* ᴱ16:22 Other mss read *will have sorrow* ᶠ16:27 Other mss read *from the Father*

17 Jesus spoke these things, looked up to heaven, and said:

Father,
the hour has come.
Glorify Your Son
so that the Son may glorify You,
² for You gave Him authority
over all flesh;ᴬ
so He may give eternal life
to all You have given Him.
³ This is eternal life:
that they may know You,
the only true God,
and the One
You have sent—Jesus Christ.
⁴ I have glorified You on the earth
by completing the work You gave Me
to do.
⁵ Now, Father, glorify Me
in Your presence
with that glory I had with You
before the world existed.

⁶ I have revealed Your name
to the men You gave Me
from the world.
They were Yours, You gave them to Me,
and they have kept Your word.
⁷ Now they know that all things
You have given to Me are from You,
⁸ because the words that You gave Me,
I have given them.
They have received them
and have known for certain
that I came from You.
They have believed that You sent Me.
⁹ I prayᴮ for them.
I am not praying for the world
but for those You have given Me,
because they are Yours.
¹⁰ Everything I have is Yours,
and everything You have is Mine,
and I have been glorified in them.
¹¹ I am no longer in the world,
but they are in the world,
and I am coming to You.
Holy Father,
protectᶜ them by Your name
that You have given Me,
so that they may be one as We are one.
¹² While I was with them,

I was protecting them by Your name
that You have given Me.
I guarded them and not one of them
is lost,
except the son of destruction,ᴰ
so that the Scripture may be fulfilled.
¹³ Now I am coming to You,
and I speak these things in the world
so that they may have My joy
completed in them.
¹⁴ I have given them Your word.
The world hated them
because they are not of the world,
as I am not of the world.
¹⁵ I am not praying
that You take them out of the world
but that You protect them
from the evil one.
¹⁶ They are not of the world,
as I am not of the world.
¹⁷ Sanctifyᴱ them by the truth;
Your word is truth.
¹⁸ As You sent Me into the world,
I also have sent them into the world.
¹⁹ I sanctify Myself for them,
so they also may be sanctified
by the truth.

²⁰ I pray not only for these,
but also for those who believe in Me
through their message.
²¹ May they all be one,
as You, Father, are in Me and I am
in You.
May they also be oneᶠ in Us,
so the world may believe You sent Me.
²² I have given them the glory
You have given Me.
May they be one as We are one.
²³ I am in them and You are in Me.
May they be made completely one,
so the world may know You have
sent Me
and have loved them as
You have loved Me.
²⁴ Father,
I desire those You have given Me
to be with Me where I am.
Then they will see My glory,
which You have given Me
because You loved Me
before the world's foundation.

ᴬ**17:2** Or *people*   ᴮ**17:9** Lit *ask* (throughout this passage)   ᶜ**17:11** Lit *keep* (throughout this passage)   ᴰ**17:12** The one destined for
destruction, loss, or perdition   ᴱ**17:17** Set apart for special use   ᶠ**17:21** Other mss omit *one*

²⁵ Righteous Father!
The world has not known You.
However, I have known You,
and these have known
   that You sent Me.
²⁶ I made Your name known to them
and will make it known,
so the love You have loved Me with
may be in them and I may be in them.

18 After Jesus had said these things, He went out with His disciples across the Kidron Valley, where there was a garden, and He and His disciples went into it. ²Judas, who betrayed Him, also knew the place, because Jesus often met there with His disciples. ³So Judas took a company of soldiers and some temple police from the chief priests and the Pharisees and came there with lanterns, torches, and weapons.

⁴Then Jesus, knowing everything that was about to happen to Him, went out and said to them, "Who is it you're looking for?"

⁵"Jesus the Nazarene," they answered.

"I am He,"ᴬ Jesus told them.

Judas, who betrayed Him, was also standing with them. ⁶When He told them, "I am He," they stepped back and fell to the ground.

⁷Then He asked them again, "Who is it you're looking for?"

"Jesus the Nazarene," they said.

⁸"I told you I am He," Jesus replied. "So if you're looking for Me, let these men go." ⁹This was to fulfill the words He had said: "I have not lost one of those You have given Me."

¹⁰Then Simon Peter, who had a sword, drew it, struck the high priest's slave, and cut off his right ear. (The slave's name was Malchus.)

¹¹At that, Jesus said to Peter, "Sheathe your sword! Am I not to drink the cup the Father has given Me?"

¹²Then the company of soldiers, the commander, and the Jewish temple police arrested Jesus and tied Him up. ¹³First they led Him to Annas, for he was the father-in-law of Caiaphas, who was high priest that year. ¹⁴Caiaphas was the one who had advised the Jews that it was advantageous that one man should die for the people.

¹⁵Meanwhile, Simon Peter was following Jesus, as was another disciple. That disciple was an acquaintance of the high priest; so he went with Jesus into the high priest's courtyard.

¹⁶But Peter remained standing outside by the door. So the other disciple, the one known to the high priest, went out and spoke to the girl who was the doorkeeper and brought Peter in.

¹⁷Then the slave girl who was the doorkeeper said to Peter, "You aren't one of this man's disciples too, are you?"

"I am not!" he said. ¹⁸Now the slaves and the temple police had made a charcoal fire, because it was cold. They were standing there warming themselves, and Peter was standing with them, warming himself.

¹⁹The high priest questioned Jesus about His disciples and about His teaching.

²⁰"I have spoken openly to the world," Jesus answered him. "I have always taught in the synagogue and in the temple complex, where all the Jews congregate, and I haven't spoken anything in secret. ²¹Why do you question Me? Question those who heard what I told them. Look, they know what I said."

²²When He had said these things, one of the temple police standing by slapped Jesus, saying, "Is this the way you answer the high priest?"

²³"If I have spoken wrongly," Jesus answered him, "give evidenceᴮ about the wrong; but if rightly, why do you hit Me?"

²⁴Then Annas sent Him bound to Caiaphas the high priest.

²⁵Now Simon Peter was standing and warming himself. They said to him, "You aren't one of His disciples too, are you?"

He denied it and said, "I am not!"

²⁶One of the high priest's slaves, a relative of the man whose ear Peter had cut off, said, "Didn't I see you with Him in the garden?"

²⁷Peter then denied it again. Immediately a rooster crowed.

²⁸Then they took Jesus from Caiaphas to the governor's headquarters. It was early morning. They did not enter the headquarters themselves; otherwise they would be defiled and unable to eat the Passover.

²⁹Then Pilate came out to them and said, "What charge do you bring against this man?"

³⁰They answered him, "If this man weren't a criminal,ᶜ we wouldn't have handed Him over to you."

³¹So Pilate told them, "Take Him yourselves and judge Him according to your law."

"It's not legalᴰ for us to put anyone to death," the Jews declared. ³²They said this so that Jesus' words might be fulfilled signifying what kind of death He was going to die.

³³ Then Pilate went back into the headquarters, summoned Jesus, and said to Him, "Are You the King of the Jews?"

³⁴ Jesus answered, "Are you asking this on your own, or have others told you about Me?"

³⁵ "I'm not a Jew, am I?" Pilate replied. "Your own nation and the chief priests handed You over to me. What have You done?"

³⁶ "My kingdom is not of this world," said Jesus. "If My kingdom were of this world, My servantsᴬ would fight, so that I wouldn't be handed over to the Jews. As it is, My kingdom does not have its origin here."ᴮ

³⁷ "You are a king then?" Pilate asked.

"You say that I'm a king," Jesus replied. "I was born for this, and I have come into the world for this: to testify to the truth. Everyone who is of the truth listens to My voice."

³⁸ "What is truth?" said Pilate.

After he had said this, he went out to the Jews again and told them, "I find no grounds for charging Him. ³⁹ You have a custom that I release one prisoner to you at the Passover. So, do you want me to release to you the King of the Jews?"

⁴⁰ They shouted back, "Not this man, but Barabbas!" Now Barabbas was a revolutionary.ᶜ

19 Then Pilate took Jesus and had Him flogged. ² The soldiers also twisted together a crown of thorns, put it on His head, and threw a purple robe around Him. ³ And they repeatedly came up to Him and said, "Hail, King of the Jews!" and were slapping His face.

⁴ Pilate went outside again and said to them, "Look, I'm bringing Him outside to you to let you know I find no grounds for charging Him."

⁵ Then Jesus came out wearing the crown of thorns and the purple robe. Pilate said to them, "Here is the man!"

⁶ When the chief priests and the temple police saw Him, they shouted, "Crucify! Crucify!"

Pilate responded, "Take Him and crucify Him yourselves, for I find no grounds for charging Him."

⁷ "We have a law," the Jews replied to him, "and according to that law He must die, because He made Himselfᴰ the Son of God."

⁸ When Pilate heard this statement, he was more afraid than ever. ⁹ He went back into the headquarters and asked Jesus, "Where are You from?" But Jesus did not give him an answer.

¹⁰ So Pilate said to Him, "You're not talking to me? Don't You know that I have the authority to release You and the authority to crucify You?"

¹¹ "You would have no authority over Me at all," Jesus answered him, "if it hadn't been given you from above. This is why the one who handed Me over to you has the greater sin."ᴱ

¹² From that moment Pilate made every effortᶠ to release Him. But the Jews shouted, "If you release this man, you are not Caesar's friend. Anyone who makes himself a king opposes Caesar!"

¹³ When Pilate heard these words, he brought Jesus outside. He sat down on the judge's bench in a place called the Stone Pavement (but in Hebrew *Gabbatha*). ¹⁴ It was the preparation day for the Passover, and it was about six in the morning.ᴳ Then he told the Jews, "Here is your king!"

¹⁵ But they shouted, "Take Him away! Take Him away! Crucify Him!"

Pilate said to them, "Should I crucify your king?"

"We have no king but Caesar!" the chief priests answered.

¹⁶ So then, because of them, he handed Him over to be crucified.

Therefore they took Jesus away.ᴴ ¹⁷ Carrying His own cross, He went out to what is called Skull Place, which in Hebrew is called *Golgotha*. ¹⁸ There they crucified Him and two others with Him, one on either side, with Jesus in the middle. ¹⁹ Pilate also had a sign lettered and put on the cross. The inscription was:

JESUS THE NAZARENE
THE KING OF THE JEWS.

²⁰ Many of the Jews read this sign, because the place where Jesus was crucified was near the city, and it was written in Hebrew,ᴵ Latin, and Greek. ²¹ So the chief priests of the Jews said to Pilate, "Don't write, 'The King of the

ᴬ18:36 Or *attendants*, or *helpers*   ᴮ18:36 Lit *My kingdom is not from here*   ᶜ18:40 Or *robber*; see Jn 1:1,8 for the same Gk word used here   ᴰ19:7 He claimed to be   ᴱ19:11 To *have sin* is an idiom that refers to guilt caused by sin.   ᶠ19:12 Lit *Pilate was trying*   ᴳ19:14 Lit *the sixth hour*; see note at Jn 1:39; an alt time reckoning would be *about noon*   ᴴ19:16 Other mss add *and led Him out*   ᴵ19:20 Or *Aramaic*

Jews,' but that He said, 'I am the King of the Jews.'"

²²Pilate replied, "What I have written, I have written."

²³When the soldiers crucified Jesus, they took His clothes and divided them into four parts, a part for each soldier. They also took the tunic, which was seamless, woven in one piece from the top. ²⁴So they said to one another, "Let's not tear it, but cast lots for it, to see who gets it." They did this to fulfill the Scripture that says: **They divided My clothes among themselves, and they cast lots for My clothing.**ᴬ And this is what the soldiers did.

²⁵Standing by the cross of Jesus were His mother, His mother's sister, Mary the wife of Clopas, and Mary Magdalene. ²⁶When Jesus saw His mother and the disciple He loved standing there, He said to His mother, "Woman, here is your son." ²⁷Then He said to the disciple, "Here is your mother." And from that hour the disciple took her into his home.

²⁸After this, when Jesus knew that everything was now accomplished that the Scripture might be fulfilled, He said, "I'm thirsty!" ²⁹A jar full of sour wine was sitting there; so they fixed a sponge full of sour wine on hyssopᴮ and held it up to His mouth.

³⁰When Jesus had received the sour wine, He said, "It is finished!" Then bowing His head, He gave up His spirit.

³¹Since it was the preparation day, the Jews did not want the bodies to remain on the cross on the Sabbath (for that Sabbath was a specialᶜ day). They requested that Pilate have the men's legs broken and that their bodies be taken away. ³²So the soldiers came and broke the legs of the first man and of the other one who had been crucified with Him. ³³When they came to Jesus, they did not break His legs since they saw that He was already dead. ³⁴But one of the soldiers pierced His side with a spear, and at once blood and water came out. ³⁵He who saw this has testified so that you also may believe. His testimony is true, and he knows he is telling the truth. ³⁶For these things happened so that the Scripture would be fulfilled: **Not one of His bones will be broken.**ᴰ ³⁷Also, another Scripture says: **They will look at the One they pierced.**ᴱ

³⁸After this, Joseph of Arimathea, who was a disciple of Jesus—but secretly because of his fear of the Jews—asked Pilate that he might remove Jesus' body. Pilate gave him permission, so he came and took His body away. ³⁹Nicodemus (who had previously come to Him at night) also came, bringing a mixture of about 75 poundsᶠ of myrrh and aloes. ⁴⁰Then they took Jesus' body and wrapped it in linen cloths with the aromatic spices, according to the burial custom of the Jews. ⁴¹There was a garden in the place where He was crucified. A new tomb was in the garden; no one had yet been placed in it. ⁴²They placed Jesus there because of the Jewish preparation and since the tomb was nearby.

20 On the first day of the week Mary Magdalene came to the tomb early, while it was still dark. She saw that the stone had been removedᴳ from the tomb. ²So she ran to Simon Peter and to the other disciple, the one Jesus loved, and said to them, "They have taken the Lord out of the tomb, and we don't know where they have put Him!"

³At that, Peter and the other disciple went out, heading for the tomb. ⁴The two were running together, but the other disciple outran Peter and got to the tomb first. ⁵Stooping down, he saw the linen cloths lying there, yet he did not go in. ⁶Then, following him, Simon Peter came also. He entered the tomb and saw the linen cloths lying there. ⁷The wrapping that had been on His head was not lying with the linen cloths but was folded up in a separate place by itself. ⁸The other disciple, who had reached the tomb first, then entered the tomb, saw, and believed. ⁹For they still did not understand the Scripture that He must rise from the dead. ¹⁰Then the disciples went home again.

¹¹But Mary stood outside facing the tomb, crying. As she was crying, she stooped to look into the tomb. ¹²She saw two angels in white sitting there, one at the head and one at the feet, where Jesus' body had been lying. ¹³They said to her, "Woman, why are you crying?"

"Because they've taken away my Lord," she told them, "and I don't know where they've put Him." ¹⁴Having said this, she turned around and saw Jesus standing there, though she did not know it was Jesus.

¹⁵"Woman," Jesus said to her, "why are you crying? Who is it you are looking for?"

ᴬ**19:24** Ps 22:18 ᴮ**19:29** Or *with hyssop* ᶜ**19:31** Lit *great* ᴰ**19:36** Ex 12:46; Nm 9:12; Ps 34:20 ᴱ**19:37** Zch 12:10 ᶠ**19:39** Lit *100 litrai*; a Roman *litrai* = 12 ounces ᴳ**20:1** Lit *She saw the stone removed*

Supposing He was the gardener, she replied, "Sir, if you've removed Him, tell me where you've put Him, and I will take Him away."

[16]Jesus said, "Mary."

Turning around, she said to Him in Hebrew, *"Rabbouni!"*[A]—which means "Teacher."

[17]"Don't cling to Me," Jesus told her, "for I have not yet ascended to the Father. But go to My brothers and tell them that I am ascending to My Father and your Father—to My God and your God."

[18]Mary Magdalene went and announced to the disciples, "I have seen the Lord!" And she told them what[B] He had said to her.

[19]In the evening of that first day of the week, the disciples were gathered together with the doors locked because of their fear of the Jews. Then Jesus came, stood among them, and said to them, "Peace to you!"

[20]Having said this, He showed them His hands and His side. So the disciples rejoiced when they saw the Lord.

[21]Jesus said to them again, "Peace to you! As the Father has sent Me, I also send you." [22]After saying this, He breathed on them and said,[C] "Receive the Holy Spirit. [23]If you forgive the sins of any, they are forgiven them; if you retain the sins of any, they are retained."

[24]But one of the Twelve, Thomas (called "Twin"), was not with them when Jesus came. [25]So the other disciples kept telling him, "We have seen the Lord!"

But he said to them, "If I don't see the mark of the nails in His hands, put my finger into the mark of the nails, and put my hand into His side, I will never believe!"

[26]After eight days His disciples were indoors again, and Thomas was with them. Even though the doors were locked, Jesus came and stood among them. He said, "Peace to you!"

[27]Then He said to Thomas, "Put your finger here and observe My hands. Reach out your hand and put it into My side. Don't be an unbeliever, but a believer."

[28]Thomas responded to Him, "My Lord and my God!"

[29]Jesus said, "Because you have seen Me, you have believed.[D] Those who believe without seeing are blessed."

[30]Jesus performed many other signs in the presence of His disciples that are not written in this book. [31]But these are written so that you may believe Jesus is the Messiah, the Son of God,[E] and by believing you may have life in His name.

21 After this, Jesus revealed Himself again to His disciples by the Sea of Tiberias.[F] He revealed Himself in this way:

[2]Simon Peter, Thomas (called "Twin"), Nathanael from Cana of Galilee, Zebedee's sons, and two others of His disciples were together.

[3]"I'm going fishing," Simon Peter said to them.

"We're coming with you," they told him. They went out and got into the boat, but that night they caught nothing.

[4]When daybreak came, Jesus stood on the shore. However, the disciples did not know it was Jesus.

[5]"Men,"[G] Jesus called to them, "you don't have any fish, do you?"

"No," they answered.

[6]"Cast the net on the right side of the boat," He told them, "and you'll find some." So they did,[H] and they were unable to haul it in because of the large number of fish. [7]Therefore the disciple, the one Jesus loved, said to Peter, "It is the Lord!"

When Simon Peter heard that it was the Lord, he tied his outer garment around him[I] (for he was stripped) and plunged into the sea. [8]But since they were not far from land (about 100 yards[J] away), the other disciples came in the boat, dragging the net full of fish. [9]When they got out on land, they saw a charcoal fire there, with fish lying on it, and bread.

[10]"Bring some of the fish you've just caught," Jesus told them. [11]So Simon Peter got up and hauled the net ashore, full of large fish—153 of them. Even though there were so many, the net was not torn.

[12]"Come and have breakfast," Jesus told them. None of the disciples dared ask Him, "Who are You?" because they knew it was the Lord. [13]Jesus came, took the bread, and gave it to them. He did the same with the fish.

[14]This was now the third time[K] Jesus appeared[L] to the disciples after He was raised from the dead.

[A]20:16 *Rabbouni* is also used in Mk 10:51   [B]20:18 Lit *these things*   [C]20:22 Lit *He breathed and said to them*   [D]20:29 Or *have you believed?* (as a question)   [E]20:31 Or *that the Messiah, the Son of God, is Jesus*   [F]21:1 The Sea of Galilee; *Sea of Tiberias* is used only in John; Jn 6:1,23   [G]21:5 Lit *Children*   [H]21:6 Lit *they cast*   [I]21:7 Lit *he girded his garment*   [J]21:8 Lit *about 200 cubits*   [K]21:14 The other two are in Jn 20:19-29.   [L]21:14 Lit *was revealed* (see v. 1)

¹⁵When they had eaten breakfast, Jesus asked Simon Peter, "Simon, son of John,[A] do you love[B] Me more than these?"

"Yes, Lord," he said to Him, "You know that I love You."

"Feed My lambs," He told him.

¹⁶A second time He asked him, "Simon, son of John, do you love Me?"

"Yes, Lord," he said to Him, "You know that I love You."

"Shepherd My sheep," He told him.

¹⁷He asked him the third time, "Simon, son of John, do you love Me?"

Peter was grieved that He asked him the third time, "Do you love Me?" He said, "Lord, You know everything! You know that I love You."

"Feed My sheep," Jesus said. ¹⁸"I assure you: When you were young, you would tie your belt and walk wherever you wanted. But when you grow old, you will stretch out your hands and someone else will tie you and carry you where you don't want to go." ¹⁹He said this to signify by what kind of death he would glorify God.[C] After saying this, He told him, "Follow Me!"

²⁰So Peter turned around and saw the disciple Jesus loved following them. That disciple was the one who had leaned back against Jesus at the supper and asked, "Lord, who is the one that's going to betray You?" ²¹When Peter saw him, he said to Jesus, "Lord—what about him?"

²²"If I want him to remain until I come," Jesus answered, "what is that to you? As for you, follow Me."

²³So this report[D] spread to the brothers[E] that this disciple would not die. Yet Jesus did not tell him that he would not die, but, "If I want him to remain until I come, what is that to you?"

²⁴This is the disciple who testifies to these things and who wrote them down. We know that his testimony is true.

²⁵And there are also many other things that Jesus did, which, if they were written one by one, I suppose not even the world itself could contain the books[F] that would be written.

[A]**21:15-17** Other mss read *Simon, son of Jonah*; Mt 16:17; Jn 1:42   [B]**21:15-17** Two synonyms are translated *love* in this conversation: *agapao*, the first 2 times by Jesus (vv. 15-16); and *phileo*, the last time by Jesus (v. 17) and all 3 times by Peter (vv. 15-17). Peter's threefold confession of love for Jesus corresponds to his earlier threefold denial of Jesus; Jn 18:15-18,25-27.   [C]**21:19** Jesus predicts that Peter would be martyred. Church tradition says that Peter was crucified upside down.   [D]**21:23** Lit *this word*   [E]**21:23** The word brothers refers to the late first century Christian community.   [F]**21:25** Lit *scroll*